Faith Parenting

Parents *Like You* Can Grow Faith Kids

by
Steve Wamberg
and John Conaway

Foreword by
Norm Wright

Faith Parenting

Parents *Like You* Can Grow Faith Kids

Age-level tips in chapters 12-19 were adapted from *Reach Every One You Teach* by Rosann Englebretson and Marlene LeFever with Steve Wamberg. Copyright © 1998 by Cook Communications Ministries. Used by permission.

All Scripture quotations, unless otherwise stated, are from The Holy Bible: New International Version. Copyright © 1973, 1978, 1984 by International Bible Society. Used by permission of Zondervan Publishing House. All rights reserved.

Editor: Linda Vixie
Cover design: Koechel Peterson
Interior design: ImageStudios

About the authors:
With over fifty years of church ministry experience between them, Steve Wamberg and John Conaway write as church "insiders"—people who love God, His church, and His people. Steve is an ordained minister who also has experience as a curriculum writer, musician, puppeteer, church renewal specialist, and Sunday School teacher. John first became involved in church ministry by helping his missionary mother handle Sunday School flannel graphs when he was six years old. Since then he has served in most volunteer church positions at one time or another—especially teaching Sunday School—and for over twenty years has worked as a full-time curriculum developer.

Printed in U.S.A.
1 2 3 4 5 Printing/Year 03 02 01 99

Table of Contents

Introduction 7

SECTION ONE: Growing Faith Kids

Chapter 1: What's a Faith Kid? 21

Chapter 2: How Does the Home/Church Link Work? 33

SECTION TWO: Making the Most of Your Home/Church Link

Chapter 3: Teaching Godly Values..47

Chapter 4: Teachable Moments 59

Chapter 5: Identifying Each Child's Needs 67

Chapter 6: Anywhere and Everywhere 73

Chapter 7: Your Indispensable Partner 83

Chapter 8: Growing with Your Children 91

Chapter 9: Model Your Faith..99

Chapter 10: Be Encouraging 107

Chapter 11: How Does It Fit? 115

SECTION THREE: Age-Level Issues

Chapter 12: Toddlers and Two Year Olds 121

Chapter 13: Preschoolers (3-5 Years)...125

Chapter 14: Early Elementary Children..129

Chapter 15: Elementary Children 133

Chapter 16: Upper Elementary Children..137

Chapter 17: Middle Schoolers...141

Chapter 18: High Schoolers 145

Chapter 19: Adults 149

AFTERWORD

Chapter 20: "Keep On Keeping On" 153

Foreword

Faith Parenting—Is this a new concept? Not really. But it is presented in a new, practical, and realistic format. The illustrations are so vivid that the reader's heart and mind will be engaged and enlightened. There will be times when your response will be "I can do that," or "Why didn't I thnk of that?" The "Watch This Principle" section is the heart of this book. When these ideas are understood and implemented, there will be results!

It's a delight to recommend this resource as an aid in helping parents fulfill their calling to nurture and train their children.

H. Norman Wright
Author and
Marriage, Family & Child Counselor

Introduction

THERE'S A COMMON LINK between the home and Sunday
School: your child. When children like yours are prepared to take
their faith home, and to examine their world through the faith
they learn with others at church, miracles happen. When you—
the parent—reinforce and add to what was learned in church, you
help children develop a faith of their own.

What was the last miracle in your home? How are you con-
tributing to your child's spiritual development? How are you tap-
ping into the resources of your church and Sunday School? The
following story illustrates the kinds of miracles that can happen
when home and church work together.

Talking with Carol, Rick had no affair to confess as he packed his bags. It sure would have been easier to explain if there had been.

"Rick, then why are you leaving?"

"I can't explain it. I just need some space right now." He regretted those words the moment they left his mouth.

"Oh, come on! I might have been able to stomach that when we were nineteen. But now you're talking a mortgage and three kids—even if I don't matter anymore."

"You do matter. And I will take care of the mortgage, and your expenses, and whatever it takes for Ryan and the twins."

"It takes a dad, Rick. It takes a dad to set examples and be here as much as he can to tuck his children in at night. It takes a dad to take his boys to church and karate lessons and . . ." He would never forget Carol's face at that moment. "What about me? What did I do?"

"Carol, the last thing I want is for you to blame yourself for anything. This is my problem, whatever it is, and I have to work it out." He fumbled through some papers in his work calendar. "This is where I'm staying. It's one of those longer-term business suites. The office has a great rate worked out with them. I'm not changing any numbers. Cell phone, pager, office—I'm just ten minutes away at the office or at this suite place."

"What about Ryan?"

That was the question that had kept Rick from doing anything for the months he'd been feeling this whatever-it-was in his gut. He sighed and started what he thought would be a nearly impossible negotiation.

Rick and Carol's other sons were teenagers. Rick had already talked the situation over with them. They'd worked out the details with Carol about juggling weekend visits around work and sports schedules. But Ryan was only eight. "I'd like Ryan with me as much as possible. I'd love to pick him up Friday after school and keep him until it's time for church Sunday mornings. I want to share what part of school holidays I can with him."

"So you'll come to church with him?"

"No, Carol. I have no doubt that the church will gather around you the next few months. I don't know that I can take the stares and the rumors that will likely fly."

"So you think the boys and I will enjoy them?"

"No. And I wish there were something I could do about that."

"There is. Don't go."

"It's not that simple, Carol. Fridays? Can I pick Ryan up after school? We can go to the boys' games together that way, at least. Will it work for you?"

She nodded and looked at the floor.

He snapped his suitcase shut. "I'll load this and come back in so we can talk with Ryan."

That conversation was a blur. Ryan took the news about as well as any eight year old could. Rick explained this wasn't a divorce, that Ryan wasn't the cause, all the stuff the experts say you need to do to give a kid some equilibrium in the situation.

If Rick hadn't taught his sons to look people straight in the eye when they were talking, it would have been a lot easier.

"So, Dad, when are you coming home?" Maybe he was treating this as if his dad were going on an extended business trip. Maybe Rick was, too.

"I don't know, Son. But I'll always be just a few minutes away. And I'll come for you Fridays and be at your soccer games and . . ."

"Okay, Dad," he cut in. Rick saw fire and desperation all at once in the boy's eyes and realized he'd put them there. He had to get out.

Working details out at the school—and at work, for that matter—to become a joint-custody home was easier than he expected. People seemed used to dealing with this kind of situation. There were sympathetic looks, and a couple of people made themselves available to "talk things over." Even Carol was cooperative once she saw he wasn't becoming a deviant or a criminal.

That was last October. To this day, Rick can't tell you how he used his "space" much differently than he could have used the space at home. He didn't search out a quick fling with a coworker. He didn't drink himself into oblivion. He focused on work, sat alone in the suite on weeknights, and lived for Fridays. He went into work early so he'd be waiting for Ryan the moment he was out of school. They'd hit a fast-food joint and then be off to one of his brothers' games.

Still, for the first time Rick understood why holidays depress some people. Thanksgiving he volunteered at a soup kitchen to pass the time until Friday. He went to Ryan's Christmas program at ﹍ ﹍nd sat in back. He stood around with Carol and the boys ﹍minutes after the program but didn't feel comfortable going to the fellowship hall for the cookies and punch afterward.

He didn't feel comfortable not going home with them, either.

He took Ryan and his brothers after they spent Christmas Eve with Carol and her family. They had a great time for a couple of days. He worked it out with Carol and the office to spend New Year's Eve and the following two days with Ryan, too, while their teenagers were at a church retreat.

New Year's Eve fell on Sunday. Since Rick was taking Ryan for a few days, he and Carol reversed their usual schedules. She kept him Friday and Saturday, and Rick picked him up at church.

He pulled up to the curb at the front of the church just as Sunday School was letting out. He saw Norm Mills walking with Ryan. Norm and Jeri Mills taught Ryan's Sunday School class. When Norm saw Rick, he waved. Ryan ran toward the car. Rick stepped around the car to the curbside for Ryan's hug and waved back at Norm.

He'd barely made it back into the driver's seat when Ryan pulled out something about the size of a greeting card. "Hey, Dad, I made this really cool New Year's gift for you."

"New Year's gift, huh? You

didn't spend enough on me at Christmas?"

"Look at it!"

It was a calendar with Ryan's picture on it.

"And, Dad, that's our memory verse from today on it, too."

It was Psalm 90:12: *Teach us to number our days aright, that we may gain a heart of wisdom.*

"I love this, Son. Thanks. I'll keep it on my desk at work."

It had been Rick's custom to quiz the boys about what they'd learned in Sunday School when he was living with them. He did what seemed natural with Ryan that day.

"So, Ryan, what did you talk about in Sunday School today?"

"We talked about the new year. We talked about what we'd do if we could do anything we wanted today."

"Really? What did you say?"

"I said, 'If I could do anything I wanted today, I'd make my dad move back in with us.'" Then a concerned look came over his face. "Now, Dad, I understand I can't make you do anything. They just asked what I wanted. But I'm praying that you'll come back home anyway. So are Grandpa Norm and Mrs. Mills."

"Fair enough. Umm, where do you want to go for lunch?"

They ate way too much junk food the next few days. They watched bowl games. They were so inspired by what they saw on the screen that they bought a football and tossed it around in the park, even though it was cold.

For years, Rick and Carol had made it a point to look for teachable moments—times that lent themselves to reinforcing a spiritual truth. Rick was feeling so comfortable, so "normal," this weekend that he fell back into the pattern at one point in the Rose Bowl game.

"Hey, Ryan, did you see how the coach calls in the plays and the quarterback runs them? That's kind of like God and us. God sees everything we need to do, and if we're listening, He'll tell us what to do."

"Did God tell you to leave Mom?"

Rick felt as if the air had been knocked out of him. "Well . . . no . . . I know He wouldn't tell me to do that."

"Then why did you?"

For a moment or two Rick could say nothing. This teachable-moment thing just wasn't working, and he knew why. "The truth is, Ryan, I've been having trouble hearing what God is telling me these days . . . and I just needed some time to be away from everything, to try and sort it out."

"Well, maybe you just need some new batteries in your head-set," Ryan said thoughtfully.

"Batteries!" chuckled Rick. "I knew I was forgetting some-thing!" The tension was eased temporarily.

The weekend was great, and over too soon.

"Okay, Dad, remember to put the calendar on your desk." Ryan grabbed his backpack as Rick left him at the house.

"Absolutely, Son."

Then he stopped moving. "Dad, can I pray with you before I leave?"

"Sure. I'll start." Rick thanked God for Ryan, his brothers, his mom, and a new year.

Then Ryan said the prayer that Rick found out later had been his litany for the weeks his dad had been away. "God, I need my dad at home. So does Mom. So do my brothers. Bring him home, willya please? Please, Jesus? Amen."

Rick reached over and squeezed Ryan's shoulder. "Thanks, Ryan."

Ryan turned to his dad for a long hug. Then he let himself out of the car. Carol greeted him at the door. She waved as the car pulled away.

Ryan ran into the kitchen at his usual breakneck pace. "Mom, I'm hungry!"

"Didn't your father feed you?" she asked as she got out bread, peanut butter, and jam.

"Yeah, we had burgers," Ryan said as he sat down at the kitchen table and began opening his backpack, "but that was a long time ago."

"What have you got in there?"

"It's a gift for you." Ryan pulled it out of his backpack. "It's a calendar with my picture on it. And a Bible verse."

Carol read the verse aloud. "'Teach us to number our days aright, that we may gain a heart of wisdom.' What does it mean to number our days?"

"I think it means to keep track of the days in our life."

"Why does God want us to do that?"

With a twinkle in his eye, Ryan suggested, "So we'll know

when our birthdays are?"

"Well, I'm sure that is important," Carol answered with a smile, "but there's another reason. God decides how many days we have here on earth, and He wants us to make the most of them."

"How many days did He give me?" Ryan wondered.

"Well, nobody knows how long he or she will live. That's why God tells us to number our days and make the most of them." Carol put the sandwich in front of Ryan. "We are being wise when we do that."

"Thanks, Mom. Can I have another sandwich?"

"Honey, you never eat two!"

"Well, since I don't know how many more times I'll be able to eat your sandwiches, I figure I'd better eat all I can today!"

Carol laughed and cleared a place on the counter for the calendar. "Ryan, I'll put this right here so I remember to number my days too, okay?"

Rick looked at that calendar every day at work. He brought it home with him for the weekends. The verse haunted him. Ryan's picture reminded him of what he was missing.

What he'd been looking for was at home.

Rick remembered waking up in a cold sweat eight, maybe ten, years before. He was panicked. The whole "Is this what I'm supposed to be doing with my life?" scenario played out in his head. All the "What ifs?" started burning in his gut. What if I'd taken the promotion and moved the family to the coast? What if I'd married my high school sweetheart instead of waiting through college to find Carol? What if I lose my job? Who would hire me? Am I worth what I think I am on the open market?

For years these thoughts troubled him, until a few days before Valentine's Day when Rick knew what mattered again. He asked Carol out for dinner. They really talked. They took a long walk. He told her he understood her reluctance to take him back. He asked her forgiveness.

It was early March when Carol and Rick walked on either side of Ryan into his Sunday School classroom for an early visit to Norm and Jeri Mills.

"We need to thank you." The words didn't come easily from Rick that day.

Norm and Jeri furrowed their brows together almost in unison. Some people say years of marriage will do that to you. Jeri finally spoke up. "For what?"

"Hey, Ryan, go check on your older brothers for a minute. Make sure they're sitting where they need to be."

"Okay, Dad!"

"The calendars . . . the New Year's calendars. I'd look at mine every day at work. I'd see Ryan, I'd see the verse, and I started missing my family. There was no way I was spending my time wisely being apart from them." Rick looked at the floor.

"And when he asked to come back, I was ready to let him suffer and beg to see if he really meant it." Carol never was one to mince words. "But that wouldn't have been a wise use of time either—and I've been reminded of that every day this year."

Rick cleared his throat. "We're not out of the woods yet. We've got a lot to work out, especially me. We start meeting with the pastor this Tuesday. But we'll be working it out together. So . . . thanks. Really."

Norm was getting misty. "You know, Ryan's been praying for this for quite awhile."

"Yeah. So have you. Ryan's your biggest fan." He reached over to shake Norm's hand. Norm pulled him into an embrace.

"Right now, we are, too." Carol hugged Jeri. "Thanks for being here for him—and for us."

This miracle is a true story. We changed names and a few details. As of this writing, we don't know whether Rick and Carol have completely worked things through. But they're still dealing with their issues as a family, and Rick, Carol, and Ryan alike are quite convinced that God cares about families like theirs—and works through both home and church to help them become what He wants them to be.

We're convinced, too. You see, the home and the church have some very important people and a very important mission in common. The people are the students who are both a part of a home and part of a Sunday School class. The mission shared by home and church is to grow those students into deeper faith. The shared people and mission become what we call the home/church link—the connection between the home and church.

As we have seen in this story, the home is the strongest influence in a child's life. What happens at home colors children's perceptions of themselves, and of God. Therefore, we parents must take responsibility for the role God wants us to have in the lives of our children. We are not to give up this role and depend on the church or Christian media to nurture our children as they become Christian adults. At the same time, however, God intends us to use the many resources He has provided—including Christian books, videos, toys, and games in the home, as well as the gifted people and effective programs of the church—as sources of help, support, encouragement, and guidance.

We are not alone in our parenting task. God has given us the home/church link. The good news for all of us is that link already exists. All we need to do is learn how to use it more effectively.

How can we strengthen the home/church link? Like many things in life, it's a lot simpler—and a lot more profound—than you might think. The church and the home fill different but equally important roles in growing people of faith. The role of the church is faith teaching. The role of the home is something we call faith parenting—the subject of this book.

So let's launch this working definition: Faith parenting is a fun, effective way to teach godly values to your children—wherever you are—through family reading, personal sharing, playing, and the everyday modeling of God's Word so your children will become "faith kids."

Introduction

This book offers you insights into your role as a parent in the home/church link. (We'll also talk a lot about "faith kids.") Through stories, illustrations, and simply stated principles, you'll see ways to succeed in that role. You'll also encounter a number of ideas to help you make the most of that link for the sake of your children. (If you're a teacher as well, you'll also want to read *Faith Teaching*, a companion to this book.)

We want to help you get the most out of the home/church resources you already have. Because at the bottom line, the home/church link is not determined by a church's curriculum choice, building design, or programming. Parents like you make or break the home/church link. Parents like you communicate God's truth at home, one-on-one, in a hundred ways that teachers can't. Parents like you enlist the help of willing partners—your children's teachers—in nurturing your faith kids. Like no one else, you can help your children take what they've learned in Sunday School and apply it throughout the week—and go beyond the Sunday School lesson to deepen their faith every day.

Of course, it's always a plus when you have resources available to encourage the development of the home/church link. So we'll also offer you a few guidelines for analyzing resources such as books, games, toys, music, and videos.

We believe that, just by the act of picking up this book, you've already shown that you're a faith parent at heart. We want to encourage you in the teaching role you already have as a parent. Apart from God, you are the most significant person in your child's spiritual development. We also believe that the God who gave you the awesome role of parenting will give you what you need to fill in the blanks.

Our prayer is that this book helps fill that need.

John Conaway
Steve Wamberg
Colorado Springs, Colorado
July 1999

What's a Faith Kid? 1

START HERE: A FAITH KID IS SOMEONE OF ANY AGE who responds to a faith relationship with God through Jesus Christ—and demonstrates continued growth in that relationship.

In other words, faith kids are people who show that Jesus is alive and well in their hearts, minds, and actions—no matter what their age, no matter where they are.

Do you have any in your home?

Kids are supposed to be the ones watching their parents deteriorate. That's the order of the universe—or at least the way it should be.

But "should be" was long gone from Stan and Ellen's vocabulary. Ten short years ago, their son, Jamie, had been tearing up the soccer field. Don Ellis, Jamie's Sunday School teacher, had also been his little league soccer coach. Jamie was more of a musician than a muscle man even then, but his enthusiasm made up for the skills he lacked at first. Jamie was not only the team's most improved player that year, but also ended up as its leading scorer. He was on the honor roll at school to boot. Stan and Ellen couldn't wait for the years to come.

Just one year later, the strength began to leave Jamie's legs. It started with a few little stumbles on the stairs as Jamie ran up to his room. He couldn't run as fast or turn as sharply in soccer practice. And he seemed to be tired all the time. When Ellen saw Jamie brace himself on a table to keep from falling, she made an appointment with their family doctor. He recommended that Jamie be admitted to the hospital for a complete battery of tests. Stan and Ellen had never prayed as hard as they did that day.

The next day, Stan and Ellen both took off from work to meet with the doctor. The diagnosis was some rare cousin in the muscular dystrophy family. No one could miss its effects on Jamie. A gradual process of atrophy set in—painfully gradual. What began in his legs made its way to his shoulders and then his torso. Then over a few more years, it robbed Jamie of most of his ways to communicate. He could raise his eyebrows, blink, and mumble. That was about it. Stan and Ellen, by virtue of witnessing Jamie's deterioration, understood more than most.

So did Coach Ellis and his son Mark, a friend of Jamie's. They'd made it a point to be around Jamie for the last decade, too.

Jamie and Mark had made public decisions for Christ at the same church youth service the year Jamie played soccer. Stan and Ellen were proud of their son's choice and just as proud that Jamie caught details from Bible stories, and sometimes even sermons, that kept the adults around him shaking their heads in wonder. Jamie developed a reputation for keeping his class—and his teacher—on their toes.

Jamie knew that Jesus was his ultimate hope. There wasn't a doctor, nurse, therapist, or playmate who didn't know about Jamie and Jesus. Jamie's confidence and trust in God, even as he watched his own body fall apart, humbled his parents. It also allowed them, as they dealt with the reality of physical therapy and moving to a one-story house, to keep an eternal perspective on the whole situation.

Stan and Ellen needed that perspective. So did Jamie's friends. As the disease limited Jamie's movement in the next few years, he became a chaplain of sorts to his peers. They came to him with questions, and Jamie seemed to deliver just the right encouragement more often than not. When Jamie became less verbal, his friends still came to him just to unload. They knew they had Jamie's ear, and Jamie thrived on the interaction. Stan and Ellen welcomed them into their home. They knew that even though Jamie's physical condition wasn't normal, he was a normal teenager in every other way. Like other teens, he was working on establishing his own identity—and his relationships with peers played a big part in that process.

Jamie moved from a walker to a wheelchair the summer before he entered the high school class that Don Ellis taught. Stan and Ellen knew how much Jamie had been looking forward to being with his church buddies in that class. The room was a near legend among middle school youth. It had couches instead of chairs and tables. The artists of the class repainted the classroom walls in a new mural every school year. No doubt about it: the students "coming up" from middle school really looked forward to Sunday School in the high school room.

The problem was purely physical: the high school classroom was located up a flight of stairs. It was placed there, at the end of one wing of the building, because the location allowed for a livelier discussion and more activity.

Stan and Ellen weren't quite ready to talk with Jamie about the near impossibility of continuing in Sunday School. But they felt they owed it to Don to let him know that they weren't expecting a miracle from him, either. So Stan and Ellen approached him after church the Sunday before Jamie and his classmates would make the transition into the high school class.

"Listen, Coach." Stan still called Don "Coach" from soccer days. "We know Jamie's going to have trouble getting up the stairs to the high school class. We can't carry the wheelchair up there, and you shouldn't have to, either."

"Well, I've been thinking about asking for a classroom switch."

"But the room is so important to the teenagers. It's important to Jamie, just because of the 'high school mystique' and the furni-

ture and all. You shouldn't have to change everything for Jamie—"
Ellen's voice faded toward the end. "We're thinking we might just
take Jamie home before Sunday School from now on."

"Please. Let me talk to the kids before you make that decision.
Just give me today. Please."

Stan and Ellen shrugged. Coach was no quitter, but they still
couldn't see a way out of this one. "Okay, Coach." Stan turned to
watch Jamie making his way toward them from a conversation
with two other middle schoolers. "Just let us know. We're on our
way to Grandma's today, but we'll be home this evening, right,
Sport?"

"Better . . . be." Jamie's tone was firm, but his eyes were twinkling.

Stan explained, "Jamie wants to get back in time to watch a
soccer game on TV, and Grandma doesn't have cable TV. Talk to
you later, Coach." Don waited till the hydraulic platform lifted
Jamie and his wheelchair into the family's new van; then he waved
and walked back into the church building.

Stan and Ellen were each working on ways to let Jamie down
gently from the disappointment he'd surely feel by having to stop
going to Sunday School. Coach, in the meantime, gathered both
the middle school and high school classes together and talked
through Jamie's situation with them.

It was Mark, Coach's son and Jamie's friend, who suggested
that the students commit to carry Jamie and his wheelchair up the
steps every Sunday. The other kids agreed that was the thing to do.

Stan couldn't believe his ears when Coach called him with the news. "Coach, this is an every-Sunday deal. I mean, I don't want to set the kids up to fail. This is a big commitment."

"Stan, let's try it. The worst that can happen is that we have to come up with another plan. I have a good feeling about this one, anyway."

Stan hung up the phone. His mouth must have been hanging open, because Ellen asked what was up. When Stan relayed the news about the high school class commitment to Jamie, Ellen's knees buckled. She cried for joy right there in the kitchen.

That was three years and ten months ago.

Now, two hundred Sundays later—the kids had never once failed in their mission to Jamie. For his part, Jamie kept firing zingers to keep class discussions hot for a couple of years before the disease began to reduce his contributions. These days, Jamie would get out a "Jesus rules!" at the end of class, and not much else.

What's a Faith Kid?

Coach was waiting for his class this Sunday as was his custom. Mark helped carry Jamie to lead the high schoolers up the stairs, as had become his custom. This Sunday, Mark and Jamie joined their senior classmates in graduation caps and school colors. They'd been honored in the church service before class.

As Stan and Ellen approached the classroom, they heard the usual preclass bantering and laughter. They knocked loudly enough to be heard, and the door swung wide.

"Stan! Ellen! Come join us!" Coach and a few of the students scrambled to find seats for Jamie's parents, but they motioned that they would remain standing.

"Coach, is it okay that we brought treats?" Stan reached into a shopping bag for sodas. Ellen produced three dozen cupcakes from a container she was carrying.

"No problem here." The kids passed the sodas and cupcakes around, and the banter level rose again.

"We brought these for a reason. We're celebrating the seniors' graduation, and Jamie's graduation into the young adult class." Ellen smiled. "You know, the class that meets on the main level?"

"Jamie's got something to say to you all now." Stan wheeled Jamie into position so he could make eye contact with everyone in the room.

"Guys . . ." Jamie had to catch his breath as he looked from student to student—each one—and managed a small smile. "Coach . . ." The voice was weak, but the eyes still shone. Don smiled back and nodded for Jamie to continue.

"All of you—thanks!"

One by one, the students got up, walked over to Jamie and hugged him. When the last one walked away, Jamie rolled his head as if to build up steam and crackled, "Jesus rules!"

"Yes, He does." Stan agreed and smiled at the students. "And thank you all for reminding Ellen and me that He still does."

Recognizing a Faith Kid

It may sound as if Jamie and his friends were "super-Christians." Not really. They were just faith kids.

We opened the chapter with a working definition of faith kids. Let's revisit that quickly:

A faith kid is someone of any age who responds to a faith relationship with God through Jesus Christ—and demonstrates continued growth in that relationship. In other words, faith kids are people who show that Jesus is alive and well in their hearts, minds, and actions—no matter what their age, no matter where they are.

If we break down that definition, we find out that:

1. Faith kids come in all sizes and ages. In this book, we usually apply the term "faith kid" just to children and youth, but we know the definition also applies to us.

2. Faith kids are people "under development." Sometimes it's tough for parents to remember that their own faith kids aren't perfect, but still under construction. Instead of looking for the mythical "perfect child" here, let's look instead for a child who is showing signs of applying faith to everyday life.

3. Faith kids act their ages—for better or worse. Sorry, but middle school–aged faith kids won't act like miniature adults. But we do expect their responses and actions to show that they're more mature than preschoolers. (And, if they're faith kids, they'll want to grow and mature in response to what they know about God anyway.)

4. Faith kids are building toward, have established, or are building on a personal relationship with Jesus Christ. Your child may not have prayed the prayer of salvation just yet, but she's building a foundation toward that end through learning and applying God's Word to her everyday life. (And trust us—as parents we know how difficult it can be to wait for those "marker" events!) Faith kids who have that relationship are learning to live in response to that relationship—perhaps as simply as asking "What does Jesus want me to do?" as part of their daily decision making. That means we, as parents, need to ask that question in our own daily decisions so our children see what the process looks like.

5. Faith kids demonstrate spiritual growth. This can be exceptionally tough to discern as a parent. In fact, it can be like watching water boil—the process isn't all that exciting until you see the bubbles. Still, from time to time, you should be able to see progress in your children's actions and attitudes based on the impact of God's Word on their lives.

6. Faith kids live their faith inside and outside your home. This means you won't be the constant monitor of their spiritual

growth—but as a parent, you are more constant than any other spiritual monitor apart from the Holy Spirit. Elements of their development take place at home, as you drive your children to activities, at their schools, and at church.

These six points lead to a seventh:

7. Faith kids need the kind of spiritual development that helps them put their faith into action in everyday life. In all honesty, this requires appropriate spiritual input from both the church and the home. As you'll discover in the pages that follow, you and your child's Sunday School teacher play crucial—and distinct—roles in the home/church link.

Think about it: You know some faith kids already, don't you? They just might be the ones looking at you across the breakfast table every day. That means you're a faith parent. You hold the prime responsibility to help them grow to the next stage of maturity in faith.

And one of the best places to do that is as an active part of the home/church link, teamed with your church—specifically, your child's Sunday School teacher.

It's easier than you think. In fact, you're probably doing it already.

For Review and Discussion

Think about your children for a moment. What qualifies each of them as a "faith kid"? Why?

In you estimation, which of your children's Sunday School teachers does the best job of nurturing faith kids? What specific things let you know that?

Which aspect of being a faith kid (as defined above) would you most like to improve in yourself?

How Does the Home/Church Link Work?

2

T HE ROLES OF TEACHER AND PARENT in the home/church link are complementary, not identical. Sunday School teachers offer content in a more formal teaching setting, usually through relating a structured lesson from God's Word to everyday life. Parents illustrate biblical values in words and deeds, sometimes in "set-aside" time—but more often in relating spontaneous, every-day life to God's Word.

Remember: You're the parent. You don't have to be the Sunday School teacher—unless you *are* the Sunday School teacher.

The Sunday School teacher is your indispensable partner in the home/church link.

Tracy had developed a new term for how she felt: "slug parent."

She grimaced when she thought of how she stacked up against her friend Dana. She knew her husband, Dan, discouraged her from comparing herself with her friends. But Tracy was confronted with Dana every week: Dana was her son Steven's Sunday School teacher.

Dana's life was filled with carpools, church activities, Sunday School teaching, volunteer tutoring, a part-time job, and being a wife and mom. From all appearances, Dana did it all with aplomb. Tracy felt behind the proverbial eight ball simply being a mom. It took almost everything she had to keep up with five-year-old Steven and two-year-old Marla.

Dana was Wonder Woman. Tracy was the Blob. Tracy even tried to do her own "Dana thing" at home, writing elaborate Bible lessons she taught Steven. She managed to do it once in a row; it was an utter flop. Dana's "perfection" might have driven her insane with envy if Dana wasn't such a good friend, too.

Every Tuesday, Dana and Tracy met for an hour at the same coffee shop. It was their weekly break from their children, and both looked forward to this chance for "grown-up" talk. One Tuesday, as they settled into a booth, Tracy blurted, "You know, Dana, it's almost embarrassing to have Steven in your class."

"What do you mean?" Dana stirred the whipped cream into her hot chocolate.

"There are some weeks I feel like a total slug as a parent when

How Does the Home/Church Link Work?

I think about the quality of the hour you spend with Steven at Sunday School. You tell him most of the little things I mean to, and take the walks that I should be making time to take with him, and to be honest, your birthday cake for him made mine look puny.

"How do you do it so well for the kids in your Sunday School class and manage your brood at home?"

"I . . . I don't know. I guess I've never thought about it that way. . . . So how does Dan like his new job?"

Tracy took the verbal bait and ran with it. She was proud of her husband's promotion, so the rest of the time at the coffee shop was spent in the details of Dan's office politics.

Sunday came and Steven was treated to what seemed to be another outstanding lesson. Tuesday morning came around again, and the two coffee buddies kept their regular date.

Dana seemed more distracted than usual. "Tracy, I changed the subject of our conversation last week. I'd like to begin again."

"I don't remember what we were talking about."

"You asked me something about how I balance Sunday School teaching and everything else."

"Forget it. I was just blowing off steam."

"No, you were right," insisted Dana. "I didn't know how to handle the question last time, and I've been thinking about it all week. You know, I don't think I'm managing the balance well at all.

"Shannon introduced me as her 'overcommitted mother' to one of her teachers the other day. She even had to remind me that

Monday was my hubby's birthday—and I needed the reminder.

"You know, I love teaching Sunday School. I think I'm gifted to do it. But last Sunday I tried to look at my class a little differently. I asked myself, 'What do these kids know about the Bible that I didn't teach them?' It was eye-opening, and humbling!"

"What do you mean?"

"I'll give you an example. Our Bible story was about Jesus healing a man who had leprosy. I asked whether anyone knew what leprosy was. Your Steven piped right up with a good answer. He said he remembered it from a Bible story book you read to him."

"Well," Tracy said, "we do read a Bible story sometime during the day, usually just before bed. Then we talk about it."

"And that wasn't all," Dana went on, "Steven went on to talk about how when his grandpa went into the hospital, you prayed for him as a family, and now he's better. He linked it to Jesus healing the leper—and we hadn't even gotten to the application part of the lesson yet!

"Tracy, I want you to forgive me. Maybe at some level I've been trying to prove something. But I can't take your place as Steven's teacher—not even for one hour a week. I can do some things. I can help Steven learn how to learn in a school-like situation, with other kids. I can help him feel welcome at church. I can help him learn some basic facts. But even in that one hour with me, your teaching comes through. I'm so impressed!"

"But I haven't done anything spectacular," protested Tracy. "I'm just doing what I can to expose my kids to the Bible and help them understand what God is like. Just normal stuff."

"Keep it up, girl! It's working!"

Like you, Sunday School teachers are busy. Like you, they struggle to juggle many responsibilities and still keep their sanity. And most of them are parents, too. So they want to help you—and they appreciate your help, too.

That's why it's worth your while to team up with your child's Sunday School teacher. So say hi to that teacher. Send a card or a note. Teachers need your support, and you need theirs. If you offer that support, you just might find a lifelong ally in helping your child become a faith kid.

The roles of teacher and parent are both crucial in the home/church link. As you and your child's teacher come to a better understanding of the unique roles you play, you'll both find help and support—and the payoff will be the spiritual growth you see in your child.

What's My Assignment?

What does a parent do in the home/church link?

How about the Sunday School teacher?

Where do you draw the line between the two?

These are not simple questions to answer. It was revolutionary for Dana to be confronted with the idea that her efforts in Sunday School might be seen as competition by the parents of her classroom kids. It was just as revolutionary for Tracy to discover how effective her home-teaching practices were.

We're Sunday School teachers. We even write curricula. But before that, we're parents. Many times it's easier for us to write a lesson than it is to apply that lesson at home.

But like you, we're dedicated to making God's Word the road map for our homes. Like you, we face the task of teaching our kids right in our own homes how God's Word applies to everyday life. We learn and relearn how to teach through words and deeds. We have to remember that they're not just our children, they're God's children too. So we depend on Him for help.

As much as we love Sunday School, we know that we need to use other resources to teach well at home. We lay aside the formal lessons in exchange for family activity guides or storybooks or a wacky activity or a simple story from our own lives.

It's not so different from what you're already doing. But you can make more of your role as a faith parent.

What's your assignment as a parent in the home/church link? Perhaps one of the first and most important roles to take on is that of a teacher—but not the same kind of teacher that conducts Sunday School.

No question about it: like a Sunday School teacher, you have a crucial role in the spiritual development of your child. But your means of teaching is far different from that of the people who face your children Sunday after Sunday. Teachers in Sunday School usually offer their information through a more formal setting than you do. They usually deal with a larger group setting than you do. They use a structured lesson plan, even if it looks like a lot of "fun in the classroom."

But unlike that teacher, you can focus on the individual needs of your children. You can take moments of everyday life and apply God's Word to them. You can reinforce values day by day, wherever you are, through playing, reading, storytelling, or a creative family activity. You can respond almost instantly to their needs. Your point of reference to your children is not the class-room but their everyday lives.

Let's break this down. Both church and home, both teacher and parent, have their own unique roles in God's process of spiritual development. That's why parents and teachers alike are actively enhancing the home/church link more than ever before.

And how are they increasing the value of that connection? By· talking to each other.

It's a matter of feedback.

Make the Most of Your Feedback Loop

Feedback between the parts of the home/church link is crucial to the strength and health of that link.

The good news is this: most Sunday School lessons have a built-in feedback loop—all you have to do is use it. These lessons use a simple step-by-step structure, which follows a pattern called "the natural learning cycle":

Need—The lesson begins by establishing a student's need for

more knowledge by stimulating interest in the lesson topic and discussing it. If lessons build on one another (as is often the case in Sunday School curricula), a review of the last lesson's main point is part of this step.

Study—The lesson continues by offering new information to the student. This step expands the student's understanding of the Bible.

Application—This step demonstrates how the lesson content can be applied to everyday life. It allows the student to "practice" the Bible lesson in the safety of the classroom.

Response—This step helps the student plan to put the lesson into practice in the week to come and make a commitment to carry out that plan.

Take a close look at the natural learning cycle as outlined above. There's a built-in connection between church and home. The students "take home" the life application of the lesson content in the response step. That's the feedback from church to home. Feedback also happens through take-home papers. Those cartoons and stories can tell you a lot about what's going on in your child's Sunday School class!

Here's more good news about the feedback loop: most Sunday School teachers want to encourage your child to learn from you, too. These days, many Sunday School lessons begin with a kind of "debriefing" of the week just passed. It's a time for students to reflect on how God's Word has affected them in the last few days and to report on their success in carrying out their plan. That's the feedback from home to church. Week by week, the loop continues. The question is, Are you making the most of it?

As a parent, you can enhance the feedback loop in a number of ways:

Call, write, e-mail your child's teacher—or drop by the class-room at church—to help the teacher understand your child's home life, school situations, or special needs.

Invite the teacher to visit your home.

Talk to your children about take-home papers and crafts.

Let the teacher know about lessons that seemed to have an exceptional impact on your child.

Ask about what subject matter will be covered in the next few weeks.

Offer to assist in the Sunday School classroom or to help organize a special event.

We encourage you to add to this list from your own experience. We especially encourage you to do what you can to put the ideas into action.

Your children's teachers really want to hear from you.

Your Not-So-Hidden Partner

Remember: Your child's Sunday School teacher is your indispensable partner in the home/church link.

You owe it to your partner, then, to be sensitive to his or her perspective. If you're a Sunday School teacher as well as a parent, maybe this task isn't so tough. (Then again, it can be difficult not to relate to kids primarily as a parent if that's the role you have all week.)

Teachers are your partners in teaching faith. But while your focus is the transmission of values through everyday life experiences, their focus is to offer "faith information" through structured lessons. That doesn't mean you won't have structured learning times for your kids—but your structure for learning will be different than the Sunday School lesson.

Take the issue of prayer, for example. The teacher's approach to the topic may involve a story that illustrates the need to pray, Scripture about prayer, suggestions on how to pray, and an encouragement to pray daily. Your approach, in contrast, may begin with an experience that the child has. Maybe a relative is sick, a friend does something thoughtless, or the child is facing a challenge at school—something that you can use to bring up the need for prayer. At times like this, you can talk to your child about God and about prayer, read a Scripture verse that talks about prayer, and then pray with your child.

You can be more spontaneous. Your teaching is customized to the needs of the individual child. Your child's Sunday School teacher isn't there. God has provided this teachable moment just for you and your child.

A Sunday School teacher can provide a framework of principles and Scripture that introduces a child to prayer, that can then be honed at home, and then brought back to the classroom for more structured learning, which can then be tested on the home

How Does the Home/Church Link Work?

front—and on and on. But only you, the parent, can help produce the everyday environment that builds a faith kid.

One more time: the roles of teacher and parent in the home/church link are complementary, not identical. We believe God established it that way.

It isn't rocket science either. If you consider the chart below, you'll see how the home and church work together, in balance and harmony, to produce faith kids.

<u>CHURCH</u>	<u>HOME</u>
Goal: Development of faith kids	Goal: Development of faith kids
Systematic plan of Bible content to be taught; scheduled time and place	Serendipitous, opportunistic, "teachable moments"; topics for intentional teaching times are often in response to family experiences
Foundational principles; application appropriate to most students of a particular age level	Personal application, growing out of specific situations
Structured, planned, organized, scheduled	Flexible, fluid, spontaneous, as needed
Targeted to age-level groups	Targeted to individuals
Shaped by the church's Christian education goals	Guided by individual needs
Focuses on things that students of the same age have in common	Focuses on personal uniqueness
General, universal truths	Contextualized, personalized truths
Needs common to a group	Needs unique to an individual
Helps students plan for application	Helps students actualize application

The link from home to church begins in our children's concrete experiences at home. Some of those experiences may be directly related to what went on in their class on Sunday, but most are not. This is the realm of gradual, spontaneous spiritual development. As your child interprets these experiences more and more as a faith kid, he or she becomes a high-impact influence on a Sunday School class—and at school, among friends, on the job, and in your family.

At the bottom line, we believe the home/church link is as natural—and as necessary—as breathing. There's no need to blur the differences between church and home. You don't have to be the Sunday School teacher, and the Sunday School teacher doesn't have to become the parent.

We're not saying your home/church link is perfect. Ours have never been. Still, we know from experience that you—the parent—and your partner the Sunday School teacher already have the resources to make the home/church link work as God intended. You're probably more effective than you think.

And in the chapters to come, you'll find ways to make it work even better.

For Review and Discussion

How are you teaching Bible truths to your children? (Don't count just Bible stories or family devotions; remember conversation, playtime, and your example.) If you're like most parents, you'll discover you're doing a lot more than you thought!

How Does the Home/Church Link Work?

How do you currently engage Sunday School teachers to be your partners in the home/church link?

How might you improve the feedback loop between your home and your children's Sunday School teachers? What one thing can you do this week to make it better?

Teaching Godly Values 3

THE GOAL OF BIBLE KNOWLEDGE IS LIFE CHANGE.

The Harpers' brownstone was crowded enough before Jessica's sister Chrissie moved in.

Then it seemed ready to fall apart at the seams.

Jessica sighed as she poured herself a second cup of coffee. Her husband, Derek, rambled by, still half-asleep, as he made his way to the front porch for the Sunday paper. Jessica took another mug from a hook under the corner cabinet and poured Derek his morning eye-opener. She checked the clock: 7:45. She'd have to wake Brianna if Sunday School was in her plans today.

"Do you think I should call for Brianna?"

Derek shrugged. "Might be a good idea. She really seems to

enjoy that Sunday School class. And it gives Chrissie a chance to settle into a deep sleep without the noise."

"You know, I don't remember Chrissie being such a light sleeper when we were growing up."

"Did you snore then as you do now? Maybe you never heard her wake up."

"I don't snore!"

"How do you know whether or not you snore if you're asleep?" Derek's eyes were twinkling as he took his coffee, sat down, ruffled the sports section, and buried his nose in it.

"Brianna! If you want to go to Sunday School, get up now!"

A muffled groan came from upstairs. In Brianna's case, that was an indication that she'd be up and ready in fifteen minutes. Like clockwork, she was downstairs to grab a glass of orange juice and say, "I love you guys. See you in a few." Then she was out the door for the walk to church.

Jessica stared after her daughter. Out loud she mused, "I wonder if I should go with her."

"I'll never stop you, Babe." Derek answered her thought. "In fact, if something she learns there actually helps her get along with Chrissie better, I'll go with her myself."

"That would be kind of a miracle, wouldn't it?" They finished breakfast and drifted into the living room to watch a Sunday morning news show. Jessica had fallen asleep again on the couch when the kitchen door slammed.

"Hey, Chrissie. How was the night shift?" Derek had switched the channel to a football pregame show.

"The usual. Too much work, not enough pay." Jessica and Derek heard sounds of Chrissie rummaging through the kitchen drawers and then the click of the toaster. "Listen, I have only five hours to sleep. I know it crowds Brianna's style, but could you please remind her . . ."

"Hey, we understand. And she's trying."

"I know. We were all thirteen once." Chrissie made an appearance in the living room carrying toast and orange juice. "Someday we will all be older, or have worked ourselves to death."

Jessica gave Chrissie a knowing "older sister" look. "You know, you don't have to kill yourself hurrying to move out of here."

Derek nodded. "Yeah. Samsonite will be on your case soon to buy the bags under your eyes, Kid. Maybe you could drop back to a sixty- or seventy-hour workweek."

"What—and get a life?" Chrissie turned and called back on her way up the stairs to her room. "Thanks. I know you love me, anyway."

Derek waited until he heard the door close behind Chrissie. "Think you can talk to her about cutting back? I really believe if she'd just sleep a few more hours a day she'd be a lot happier. And that could solve a lot of the friction with Brianna."

Jessica shrugged. "I'll make my weekly pitch sometime tomorrow. Just don't hold your breath waiting for results."

They had a quiet hour until Brianna came home from church at noon. When Jessica heard the kitchen door open, she bolted from the couch and ran to keep it from slamming shut. The noise Brianna made, even though it was typical for a teenager, was really irritating to Chrissie.

But this time, Brianna caught the door herself and gently shut it. Jessica's eyebrows shot up in surprise.

"Hey, Mom. You used to go to Sunday School, right?"

Jessica nodded. "A long time ago. Why?"

"Can you work on this with me?" Brianna laid a take-home paper on the kitchen counter. The theme of the week was in a banner that spread across the second and third pages: "God loves us, so we should show love to others." There was a box marked "Memory Verse" that read, *My command is this: Love each other as I have loved you* (John 15:12).

Jessica vaguely remembered the verse. "This looks good. What is there to figure out?"

"See, Mom, we're supposed to put this into practice at home. And I have an idea. What if I worked really hard this week to keep quiet for Aunt Chrissie? That'd be one way to show love for her, right?"

"Sounds like a great idea to me."

"So remind me every now and then that I'm, like, on a mission this week, okay?"

"It's a deal."

Normally on Sunday afternoons Jessica took a stack of home decorating magazines to the living room couch and read them while Derek watched a game (or two, or three) on TV. This week, she found a Bible on the bookshelf—the same one she had taken to Sunday School all those years ago—and read John 15 and then went to the beginning of John's Gospel and started to read it through.

Chrissie ran downstairs at four o'clock. "Did Brianna come home? I didn't hear her." Then she was out the door for her swing shift job.

"She has been pretty quiet. Is she all right?" Derek looked up from the game and shifted in his chair. Then a voice came from upstairs.

"Is Chrissie gone?"

"Yes!"

The bass from Brianna's boom box rattled the ceiling within seconds. "Guess she's all right, then." Derek went back to the game on TV.

At least it helped today. Jessica was grateful for an afternoon without a confrontation about noise.

Brianna's "help" actually lasted through the week. By Friday, Chrissie did something rare: she stopped at the kitchen table and asked Jessica to sit down to talk.

"Listen, I'm really concerned about Brianna. She's been awfully quiet lately. Sometimes that means kids are getting into drugs and stuff, you know."

Jessica chortled. "Not to worry. It's Sunday School."

"What?"

"I'm serious. Brianna brought home this paper from Sunday School that talked about showing God's love to other people. Then she asked me if I thought it was a good idea if she showed God's love to you by being quiet when you were home so you could sleep."

"You're kidding." Chrissie was clearly stunned. "She's really into this. I mean, she's following through!"

"You tell me. Better yet, you tell her." Jessica nodded at Brianna walking toward the brownstone.

Chrissie walked over to the kitchen door. "Hey, you! I hear I'm part of an experiment!"

Brianna stopped in the kitchen doorway and looked to Jessica for a cue.

"The Sunday School paper thing."

"Oh, that. Well, yeah, Aunt Chrissie. I know I've been bugging you with noise the whole time you've lived with us. Last Sunday I realized that was a pretty stupid way to show I loved you and that I could really do something like the Bible says to do, so . . . hey, why are you crying?"

Chrissie hugged Brianna. The tension she'd carried visibly left as she leaned on her niece. "Thank you . . . thank you!"

Jessica began wondering what she and Derek would be wearing to church that Sunday.

<u>Watch</u> <u>This</u> <u>Principle</u>

For review here, let's repeat the principle: *The goal of Bible knowledge is life change.* That means what a child learns must be able to be put into action. That's what we mean by "godly values."

How do you think Brianna's family members felt when they discovered her changed behavior was due to her putting a Sunday School lesson into action? For starters, it mellowed their feelings about church. Brianna was encouraged when she saw that the application brought results. She received more reinforcement when she reported the results in class the following Sunday. And since she saw the results of showing love at home, she'll probably be more willing to show God's love to someone else—maybe a classmate at school.

Instilling godly values is one of the best ways to reinforce the home/church link. How can you make this principle work for you?

As a faith parent, you transmit values through opportunities that simply aren't available in a Sunday School environment. You can take advantage of everyday events and demonstrate to your children how God's Word relates to them outside the four classroom walls.

This privilege has been a part of faith parenting for a long time. When Moses was given the Law, for example, these instructions to parents were included:

These commandments that I give you today are to be upon your hearts. Impress them on your children. Talk about them when you sit at home and when you walk along the road, when you lie down and when you get up. Tie them as symbols on your hands and bind them on your foreheads. Write them on the doorframes of your houses and on your gates (Deut. 6:6-9).

The idea here is that parents have the awesome opportunity to help their children understand and apply God's Word concretely, in real-life situations—and that won't happen through an hour-long Sunday School–like family lesson, but by making the Word a part of moment-by-moment life.

You can discuss what God's Word means to you as a parent. You can talk about how God's Word influences you on the job. You can share the joy of God's creation with your child as you give God glory for His marvelous work. You can connect your child's life experiences with relevant passages of Scripture the very moment something happens.

We suggest that from the time your children are very young, you try to find materials—books, toys, games, videos, music— that communicate solid Bible content at their level. (You can even add Bible content if it isn't there. When reading picture books about animals, talk about how God made each one.) And also, at the level they can understand, talk about why that truth is important. For example, God made me, so I'm special; God takes care of me, so I don't need to be afraid.

And in the process, you'll build godly values into your child.

Teaching Godly Values

Identifying Godly Values

Recent research shows that parents like you want to instill values like the following in their children. We call them "The Spiritual Building Blocks." Notice how each one relates directly to attitudes or actions.

Bible Knowledge—The Bible contains answers to life's toughest questions. We want our children to value God's Word as a reliable guide for everyday life.

Reverence—God deserves our adoration, praise, worship, and love.

Faith—Children learn how to express their faith in God through loving actions.

Prayer—Children need the assurance that God will listen to them anytime, in any circumstance—and that they can listen to Him, too.

Wisdom—Children learn to apply their knowledge of right and wrong and to understand that actions have consequences.

Love—The better our children understand how deeply God loves them, the more willing they will be to show love to others.

Repentance—Children need to see the value of turning away from sin and toward God.

Trust—Children need to learn that they can rely on God in everyday life.

Forgiveness—As children see forgiveness in action, they will learn both how to give and to ask for forgiveness.

Honesty—Truth-telling is a mark of godly character, and children can learn how to tell the truth lovingly.

Obedience—Learning to obey household rules is good preparation for learning how to obey God's rules.

Respectfulness—As parents and children alike come to understand their own worth before God, they can better appreciate the value God builds into every person.

Commitment—We can teach our children the value of seeing tasks through to the finish and doing all things with excellence to God's glory.

Thankfulness—Instead of taking things for granted, children can develop an "attitude of gratitude" as they see God's gracious hand in every blessing.

Patience—Children aren't immune to stress, anger, or the desire for instant gratification. That's why patience is so important in everyday life.

Perseverance—Children need to learn the art of working through challenges rather than giving up when they meet the first sign of resistance.

Don't let the number of values overwhelm you. Think about them one at a time. You'll probably remember specific times when you've worked with most of these values with your children. And you'll have many more opportunities. God has put you in the position to teach and train your children better than anyone else can. As parents, we are with our children in many different settings and varied experiences—a privilege and responsibility their Sunday School teachers don't share with us.

It is the unique role of the faith parent—and that's who you are.

Teaching Godly Values

Home/Church Linking

Just as Jessica did, you can support your partner (the Sunday
School teacher) by helping your child apply the content of Sunday
School lessons to everyday life. Even though Jessica wasn't what
we'd call a Sunday School booster, she listened to Brianna and
took her seriously when she talked about her idea for showing
love to Chrissie. If Jessica was able to help Brianna work on this
godly value, think what a dedicated Christian parent can do!

Can we inject a few comments here on how to talk with your
children about Sunday School? Believe it or not, you have the
power to color your child's perception of Sunday School. For
example, when the first question a parent asks a child after
Sunday School is "Did you have fun?" what expectations are being
communicated? Over time, what will that child think is the
number one reason for going to Sunday School? We suggest that
the first question be something like "What did you learn?" This
clearly signals a parent's expectations about this time of the
week—the purpose for going to Sunday School is to learn.
("School" is not a dirty word to us!) Of course, since we believe
it's wrong to make Bible learning boring, we think a good second
question is "Did you have fun?"

We've tried to have a deliberate agenda when talking with our
kids about their Sunday School classes. We not only try to ask
what they learned, but also why that truth is important—what it
means to their everyday lives. If they bring home take-home
papers, we like to go over the materials with them, letting them

tell us what they mean. By our words and tone of voice, we try to communicate two things about Bible content: 1) What they learn from the Bible is true, and 2) What they learn from the Bible is relevant to their lives. Bible knowledge is not an end in itself. It is a means to life change.

It's easy to see how emphasizing the importance of godly values can make a difference in the lives of children. But there's another positive effect. If your children have a "content application" mindset, the link between home and church will be strengthened every time they go to church! They'll have something to talk about in class, they'll be looking for meaningful content during the class, and they'll be on the alert for chances to apply that truth in the following week. It's a clear home/church win-win!

Finally, there's another important way to use the principle: let your children know how you're applying Bible truth to your own life. In a natural way—when it fits naturally into a conversation, without turning it into a bragging or confession time—let your children hear about how the Bible makes a difference for you. Tell them about the successes and the failures. It's important that you model the fact that being a faith kid is a lifelong calling. We never stop learning and growing—and they need to see that's normal.

Teachable Moments 4

LEARN TO CAPITALIZE ON—AND CREATE—teachable moments with your children.

Kellie slammed the car door behind her at the curb of the elementary school.

Arlene Carpenter knew her daughter well enough to immediately ask, "What happened, Kellie?"

"They made the stupid announcement today about the stupid decision to not do anything at school about Christmas."

Arlene could only nod. "It doesn't seem right, does it?"

Kellie shook her head.

"But let's not let it ruin Thanksgiving break, all right? We can still have plenty of Christmas at home and church, right?"

Kellie sighed. "I guess so."

Lord, please give Kellie something special this year to celebrate Christmas. Even as she prayed, Arlene wracked her brain for an idea that could let Kellie show others how important Christmas was to her as a young Christian.

Their daughter's disgust with the school over the lack of Christmas became the key topic of discussion for Arlene and Bert Carpenter the next few days. They were stumped for ideas until Sunday—when Kellie walked out of her fourth and fifth grade Sunday School class.

"Mom! Dad! This is so cool! We decorated the classroom for Christmas like Mrs. Delehant always has us do, and then we read about this kid my age that put a sign in his window to witness to other people about Jesus! It was so neat that people began to slow their cars down to read what he had to say!

"So I talked with Mrs. Delehant and said maybe since we make Christmas decorations every year, this year I could make a Christmas sign to put in the window. What do you think?"

Bert nodded and smiled. "Kellie, I think you're on to something here! You know, it's like my putting 'Jesus IS the Reason for the Season' on the sign outside the tire store."

"Yeah, only I want to say something different."

"No problem. What are you thinking about?"

"I want to start with, 'Hey, World!' Because they need to be reminded what Christmas is all about!"

"Make the sign, Honey, and we'll see what we can do with it."

The rest of the afternoon was spent gathering materials and giving Kellie the opportunity to be an artist. She neatly outlined "Hey, World! It's Jesus' Birthday!!!" on a large piece of poster paper. She colored in the letters with markers the next day, and Arlene laminated the sign. On Tuesday, Bert mounted it on plywood. Then they all put lights around the sign.

On Wednesday, the sign had its debut on the Carpenters' front lawn. It certainly drew attention. Kellie was thrilled when a car would slow down to read the sign. "It's working! This is so cool!"

By the next Monday the local paper called to arrange an interview with Kellie. She took the opportunity to tell the reporter what Christmas meant to her and why she'd made the sign.

"Pretty impressive, Kellie. Let's get a picture of you next to the sign now—and watch for the Sunday morning edition."

That Sunday, Kellie's picture was on the front page of the lifestyle section. "Fifth Grader Reminds Neighborhood of 'The Reason for the Season'," the headline read.

And there was Kellie's sign, lettered neatly in her own hand:

"Hey, World! It's Jesus' Birthday!!!"

Arlene knew then her prayer was fully answered.

<u>Watch</u> <u>This</u> <u>Principle</u>

Here again is the principle of teachable moments: *Learn to capitalize on—and create—teachable moments with your children.*

You know how busy your children are and how many things they're involved in. For children in Christian homes, the three key places that make up their lives are home, school, and church. The home is headquarters, the place kids return to after school and church. That means the home touches every area of their lives. And the home is often the place that receives emotional fallout from the other areas of their lives. This situation is a perfect set-up for teachable moments.

What's a teachable moment? This chapter's story is a good example.

When Kellie got into the car after school, strong emotions came with her. She was mad and frustrated. She was intensely aware of the issues that were driving those emotions. Her mother knew that her response to Kellie was critically important. It was what we call a teachable moment.

Kellie's parents were able to channel her strong feelings into a project that Kellie will never forget. Bert and Arlene lived out their faith in God and their support of their daughter in the planning, making, and placement of Kellie's Christmas sign. Kellie's Sunday School teacher, Naomi, used a story in a structured lesson to provide an example for Kellie's action (although Naomi might not have believed at first that any of her students would follow the lead of the boy in the story).

Bert, Arlene, and Naomi alike were aware of Kellie's distress about the lack of Christmas at her school. Each of them worked to help Kellie apply her faith constructively to respond to the situation.

What do you think would have happened if Kellie's parents had come up with the idea of the lawn sign a week earlier? We don't think she would have been thrilled with the idea. But because the idea was hers and because it was energized by her own strong feelings, Kellie learned things about herself, about God, about her parents—and a lot of other things she wouldn't have learned any other way.

Home/Church Linking

So how do you make the principle of teachable moments work better in your own part of the home/church link?

First, pay close attention to what your children are saying verbally and nonverbally. Pay special attention to your children's emotions. (A slammed door may indicate the need for a follow-up question, for example.) How can a child's anger or frustration be an opening to talk about Jesus? How about feelings of sadness or hurt? How about times of joy and celebration? Before events erupt, some parents acquire Christian children's books or videos that relate to specific topics. Then, when those topics come up, they're prepared with something that can help their child to see God's perspective on that situation. And don't worry about having a perfect lesson prepared. It's more important to respond immediately, while the experience is fresh in the child's mind. Your sincerity and caring at that moment are more important than delivering a carefully formed lesson.

Second, capitalize on teachable moments to remind yourself and your kids that their Christian faith has practical application at home, at school, at church—wherever they are. It matters to God what they do, what they say, how they feel, and what they experience. The long-term goal of using teachable moments is not that your kids have a lot of information about God but that they learn to look at everything through God's eyes. And that's not a one-time lesson; it's a lifetime process.

Third, keep in touch with your children's Sunday School teachers. Don't be afraid to ask them how things are going at Sunday School for your children—or to give them insights into what's going on in your children's lives at home. For example, when John's daughter was very young, her teacher could always tell when John was out of town on a business trip because her emotions affected her behavior. So when the teacher was told about those trips ahead of time, everyone knew what to expect—and everyone coped a lot better!

Fourth, take the initiative in creating teachable moments. For example, when a child is going to school for the first time or trying out for a sports team, or the family is moving, we don't have to wait for strong emotions to happen. We can anticipate them and prepare for them by creating our own teachable moments. Look for books, videos, toys, games, or other resources that can help you prepare your children for issues they will face. You won't prevent the emotions from happening—change always brings a degree of stress—but your kids will function better during the stress if you've helped them prepare for it.

One more thing: help your children to understand more of your life beyond the home context too. Bert's statement about the sign in front of his tire shop was a big affirmation of Kellie's idea. Let them know about your work, why you chose the hobbies you have, and something about your "favorites." You'll set the example for your children to integrate their faith into their everyday lives—and your relationships will be the richer for it.

Identifying Each Child's Needs

5

Each child is different, so each requires a unique approach.

The focus of a home lesson is one individual at a time. The focus of a Sunday School lesson is on groups of individuals.

When both church and home keep their focus, children can focus, too.

Jerry and Judy Sloan are the proud parents of identical twin seven-year-old boys, Jeff and Josh. They'd heard their sons were the live wires of Tom Cody's Sunday School class, and they believed it.

So they weren't surprised when Tom sidled toward them after

church one Sunday. "I think today's Sunday School lesson confused Josh a bit. The class time really didn't allow for his questions. Do you think you could talk with him about the difference between the church as a building and the church as people?"

"No problem. How did Jeff seem to do with the idea, by the way?" Jerry smirked as though he anticipated the answer.

"You know, Jeff seemed to catch on pretty quickly today."

Judy giggled. "We've found out that the boys may look alike, but that they sure don't handle information the same way."

Jerry nodded. "Jeff's our 'idea boy.' Josh can tackle anything hands-on. But the crossover between them has yet to develop. So let me get this straight: we need to help Josh understand the difference between the church as a building and the church as people, right?"

"That's about the size of it."

"What was the Bible passage you used?"

Tom showed them the Sunday School take-home paper. It was an introduction to the idea that the church is the body of Christ. The theme verse was 1 Corinthians 12:27: *Now you are the body of Christ, and each one of you is a part of it.*

Tom looked back and forth between the Sloans. "I know metaphors can be tricky for seven year olds. If it's still a problem by next Sunday, I'll spend some more time with Josh and try to explain it again. Thanks."

"Hey, we're in this Bible learning thing together. Thank you for letting us know."

Identifying Each Child's Needs

The Sloans made their way to their traditional fast-food drive-through with Jeff and Josh. Kids' meals in hand, they drove to a park not far from their home and found an empty picnic table. After a quick round of "Rock, Paper, Scissors," Josh won the privilege of saying grace. Judy distributed the food and the ketchup for the fries. Following tradition, Jerry took the kids' meal toys and put them in his pocket until the boys had finished their lunches. Then with a deep breath, Jerry pursued the conversation.

"So, guys, what did you learn in Sunday School today?"

Jeff shrugged the "no big deal" shrug. "We learned that the church is the body of Christ."

Josh frowned. "Yeah, and I don't get it."

"What part don't you get?" Jerry needed to find some point he could clarify.

Josh thought for a minute. "All of it."

"Like what, Son?"

"I don't see how a building can become a body. Especially Jesus' body."

"You know something, Josh? I don't either. See, the 'church' that is talked about in the Bible means 'people'—not a building."

Josh furrowed his brow. "So how do people become one body? They're a bunch of different bodies!"

Judy joined in. "But when people work together and do all the things that Jesus wants us to, it's like we become one body working together."

"So why do we call the building the church?"

"That's a good question, Buddy. All I can figure is that the people who are the church spend so much time in the building that we end up calling the building 'the church.' Maybe we shouldn't, but we do."

Jeff nodded toward his brother. "So do you get it now?"

Josh worked his tongue in his mouth a few seconds. "I think so. The church isn't a building. It's a whole Jesus-loving gang!"

Jerry called Tom with the good news that afternoon.

<u>Watch</u> <u>This</u> <u>Principle</u>

Identifying children's needs is crucial to successful spiritual development. It's just as important to the home/church link, too. Let's review: *The focus of a home lesson is one individual at a time. The focus of a Sunday School lesson is on groups of individuals.*

Now, here's the payoff: when both church and home keep their focus, children can focus, too.

Did you ever feel overwhelmed as a student? Maybe it was in high school calculus or trigonometry. (At least those were the classes that overwhelmed us!) You walked in, sat down, looked at the book, realized you didn't understand it, listened to everyone else in the room talk, realized you didn't understand them either—and panicked.

If you had a good teacher, you were encouraged to stick around. Maybe you'd learn something in the class sessions just by being there. If you had a really good teacher, you found yourself in one-on-one sessions with someone who knew the subject and could answer the questions that couldn't be covered in class.

Sometimes your children will feel that same panic about faith lessons at home or at Sunday School. It isn't that they're woefully behind the other kids. In fact, you'll likely discover that your own children switch places in the "panicked learner seat" from time to time.

If your child shows confusion about a Sunday School lesson or church sermon, you're the best one-on-one helper he has.

Sunday School is a class session based on group needs. The teachers there don't ignore individuals. In fact, the best ones deliberately vary their approach throughout the class in order to reach every student. But due to their limited time, it does mean that some of their students' unique questions have to be addressed outside of class.

You can take the time, as Jerry and Judy did for Josh, to clarify a child's unique questions. As the parent, you rightly hold the position of one-on-one spiritual tutor for your child. You connect with the child in a manner that is more individualized than the Sunday School teacher could ever do. A Sunday School teacher isn't able to teach the lesson to each student individually. Likewise, it wouldn't work well for you to use a formally structured group lesson in an "up close and personal" session with a child.

Home/Church Linking

Here are a few hints for customizing your faith parenting to each child's uniqueness and how you can strengthen the home/church link in the process:

As you observe your children, try to understand their different learning styles. Does your child seem to learn best by seeing? By hearing? By touching and moving things? Does music help him learn, or does it distract him? Does he learn best alone or while interacting with others?

Remember, your role is to teach your child personalized faith lessons. There will be times when you'll want to gather the whole family for a group learning activity, but your most effective sessions will be when you can focus on one child at a time.

If you sense your child needs more individual attention in discussing an issue that wasn't resolved in the Sunday School class, work with your child one-on-one to resolve the issue.

In some cases, you might ask the Sunday School teacher to take some one-on-one time with your child to talk further about a question, either before class or afterward. But remember that his or her time is limited for this kind of discussion. The point here is that it pays to maintain contact with your child's Sunday School teacher. That teacher is your ally!

If both you and the teacher actively engage your proper focuses as partners in spiritual development, the potential for faith kid development is staggering. (And your relationship with that teacher is a great illustration of how people work together as the body of Christ.)

Anywhere and Everywhere

6

FAITH PARENTING CAN HAPPEN IN virtually any location—and at any time.

Becky and Jack were like a lot of parents. They were trying to raise kids of faith and felt the odds were against them.

Brandon, their eleven-year-old son, had come home with an eyeful from a magazine at his best friend's house. It had been left in the family's den. The magazine didn't peddle outright pornography but offered suggestions about "driving a partner wild" and had photographs that just weren't wholesome. This article was among several others on diet and health for men, which seemed to be the bulk of the magazine's content.

Brandon had immediately let his parents know what he'd

seen. "Honest! The cover said they had an article about lifting weights to get fit in six weeks!"

Jack nodded. "I believe you, Son. That kind of magazine is all over the airports when I travel. Look, now that you know about them . . ."

"I know: don't let it happen again."

Brandon left the room, then Becky let her frustration pour out. "How do we compete with what Brandon can get from some magazine one of his friend's parents leaves around? Or with TV or the Internet? How do we help him stand against temptation?"

"Seems like we need to give him options. We need to find ways that will engage him with more spiritual things. You know, maybe we could do something a little different for family devotions than a chapter from the Bible and a prayer."

"Or something extra. But what?"

Jack and Becky's eyes met. They were truly at a loss for answers. They were fairly new Christians and had been raised in homes where God was mentioned only at table grace at Thanksgiving and when someone hit his thumb with a hammer.

Becky's eyes lit up. "I know! Maybe Brandon's Sunday School lessons can help. Maybe we can tie in the theme throughout the week or something. . . . I'll talk with Susan right after church this Sunday."

Becky made her way over to Susan, Brandon's Sunday School teacher, in the church foyer, just as she'd planned.

"Susan, Jack and I want to follow up Brandon's Sunday School lessons at home."

Anywhere and Everywhere

"Becky, will you repeat that? I want to make sure I heard you clearly."

"Susan, Jack and I want to follow up what you're doing with Brandon in Sunday School. We want a copy of your lesson book, or something like that, to help us reinforce what you're teaching him."

"Wow! I can't believe this!"

"Oh, I'm sorry. . . . Is it wrong for me to ask?"

"No, no, not at all! I think I'm in the middle of every Sunday School teacher's dream, that's all! I've never had a parent ask this before. It's wonderful!"

"They're not using Sunday School lessons at home? Then what do they do for family devotions?"

The question seemed to take Susan by surprise. After a brief pause, Susan looked at Becky quizzically and shifted the course of the conversation.

"Becky, can I ask you a few questions?"

"Sure."

"What do you think people do for family devotions?"

"I imagine they'd pray. Probably they'd have some Bible reading. We do, anyway. I think it would really help the kids to have something that's designed just for them, though. That's why I thought I'd start with Brandon's Sunday School lessons. They'd fit his age and interest, and he'd be hearing the same thing all week."

"Becky, what did you do for family devotions when you were growing up?"

Becky gave a slight shrug and looked at the floor. "We didn't have any. I had no idea that a home could be Christian until a few years ago when Jack and I tried this church out on a Christmas Eve. We kept coming back. We both asked Jesus into our hearts not long after that. We really want to do the right thing for Brandon.

"But neither of us have real family experience to know what devotions with Brandon should look like. We just know we need to start somewhere, so I figured maybe the stuff you're teaching in Sunday School might work."

"Well, it might. But you'd have to revise it a lot to have it work at home as it does here. You see, they write Sunday School lessons for groups. They also tend to write them for structured time—maybe more structured than you'd like to be at home. May I make a suggestion?"

"Please!"

"I don't want you to give up on following through with the Sunday School lesson. Brandon should come home with an idea of something he'll put into action based on that week's lesson. If you'd ask him to tell you what that is right after church each Sunday, and then encourage him to follow through, that would really help."

Becky started jotting down some notes.

"Brandon also brings a take-home paper with him each week. That paper usually has a story or two, some ideas for Bible reading through the week, and even activities that will either reinforce what he heard that Sunday or set him up for the next Sunday's lesson. If you want a tie-in with Sunday School, that's probably your best resource."

"That's the story paper with the color picture on the front?"

"That's right."

"You know, Jack or I occasionally read a story in that paper with Brandon, but we haven't looked at much else in it."

"Don't feel bad about that. I don't look at Jesse's every week, and as a Sunday School teacher I should know better."

"You're sure that's better than your lesson book?"

Susan nodded. "Absolutely. Because my lesson book is designed for groups, a lot of the activities just won't translate to the individual sessions you could have with Brandon at home. It's great for teaching general principles. But Brandon probably needs a different kind of resource for the home environment.

"See, at home you can really dig into individual questions Brandon has that might never get answered in Sunday School. You can take whatever time you need, keep your session really short, or take advantage of some on-the-spot situations that you think would teach Brandon something important about God.

"Maybe it would help for you to think about it like this: At Sunday School we start with the content of God's Word and try to give Brandon an example or two of how to apply it every day. Time forces us to limit the application. But at home you can start with any number of life situations and show Brandon how God's Word applies to them. You don't have to be limited to one or two a week.

"The kind of spiritual teaching you do really depends upon where you are. You'll do something different after dinner than you will spur-of-the-moment when there's a lesson to be taught. I do something entirely different in Sunday School than I do at home. My kids need something a lot less structured than what could happen in a classroom.

"For example, we use devotions from devotional books written especially for children every day, either at breakfast or after the evening meal. There are a bunch of good books available for that."

Becky was beginning to feel a little overwhelmed. "Can you show me where to find them?"

"Sure. Becky, one more thing. We do a special family night every Thursday. There's a whole line of books that explain how to put that night of activity together. The nights are a lot of fun, and the activities are just right for the family. They're not designed to be like Sunday School at all. The Bible lesson and prayer are still there, but the time is more personal than we could ever be here in class.

"Tell you what. Are you busy Tuesday for lunch?"

Anywhere and Everywhere

"Not right now."

"Can you meet me at the mall around 11:30? There's a Christian bookstore there that has this kind of material. I can show you examples of everything we've talked about. I'd be happy to chat with you about what might work for you, Jack, and Brandon at home. Everything you do there can only help me at Sunday School."

Becky had never imagined the resources available for family faith building. She and Susan browsed through the bookstore. Susan was a wealth of information and became almost as excited watching Becky make discoveries on the shelves as Becky was herself.

Becky brought home a devotional book written for kids Brandon's age, a family night activities guide—and the reassurance that she and Jack weren't alone in the mission to raise a child with Christian values.

Watch This Principle

This principle is really pretty simple: *Faith parenting can happen in virtually any location—and at any time.*

One of the most valuable lessons Becky learned from Susan's example is that what works at Sunday School wouldn't be as effective at home—because the situations at church and home are distinctly different.

Sunday School has to focus on group learning. Home lessons can focus more on individual questions and needs. Sunday School has to deal with general principles of God's Word. Home lessons can deal with more specific life applications of God's Word.

(For a complete table on how Christian education strategies tend to vary according to home or church location, refer to page 41.)

So don't feel that you ever have to blur the line between the home and church. God has called you to be a parent. Even if you're a Sunday School teacher at church, you'll want to shift gears to a more personalized and less structured approach for the sake of your children when you're at home.

Home/Church Linking

Letting the location drive the appropriate faith development strategy is crucial to the health of the home/church link. Here are some hints to make this principle work to its fullest for you:

Recognize the distinct advantages of spiritual teaching at home that just aren't possible at Sunday School. Your opportunities to use everyday situations to reinforce God's Word far exceed a teacher's opportunities at Sunday School. Your role as a parent naturally offers insights into a child's spiritual life that a Sunday School teacher simply won't have. That being said, remember that Sunday School has a crucial role and specific strengths to bring to the home/church link too.

Find and use resources that could enhance your teaching at home. For example, use your child's Sunday take-home papers to their best advantage. Seek out home devotional products—storybooks, family activity guides, games—that will help God's Word come alive for your kids in effective, fun ways. (For example, we recommend the books and family resources published by Heritage Builders™.)

You may be a first-generation Christian adult. That's great! Ask someone where you can find Christian videos, music, games, toys, and books to help you and your family on the journey to a deeper faith. Start with a friend at church. Use the telephone directory. But find out what's there to help you in your mission to be a faith parent.

You're a crucial part of the home/church link. Sunday School teachers have curricula with lots of ideas for the classroom. Parents need resources too. For the home/church link to work best, the church must be the church and the home must be the home. Each has a God-ordained role to play in spiritual development. Each must take up its unique role in that process for the successful growth of faith kids.

Your Indispensable Partner

7

LIKE THE TWO WINGS OF AN AIRPLANE, home and church must be connected in order for a child to soar spiritually.

Shelly Burns never had as much fun in Sunday School as her four-year-old Danny was having.

Her husband, Mike, agreed. Shelly and Mike attended church services regularly but had never really been much for Sunday School as adults. They could take it or leave it, so half the time they left it. But Danny was a different story.

Every week, Danny asked if he could go to Sunday School. He really seemed to love being there. They'd learned to be ready for a retelling of the Sunday School story when Danny got into the car after church. After the story Danny would announce, "And guess what I get to do at home for the Sunday School lesson?" Then he'd tell them his "home assignment" that somehow applied what he'd learned.

They both had to admit they took genuine pleasure in watching Danny apply the lesson as well as a four year old could. His enthusiasm never seemed to waver, even if he'd missed Sunday School for two or three weeks.

There was a Sunday when Danny missed because he'd had his tonsils removed. A tonsillectomy is no big event these days. But that Friday when Mike and Shelly reviewed the release forms for the operation—the forms that remind a parent that there was a chance, however tiny, that the worst could happen—they were reminded all over again just how precious their son was to them.

Mike returned the forms to a waiting nurse. He and Shelly stood by Danny until he was wheeled away, drowsy from the anesthetic taking effect. "We'll be waiting, Champ. Love you! See you in just a few minutes!"

Mike walked over to the coffee pot in the waiting room and poured cups for Shelly and himself. Two sugars, one creamer for Shelly; black and hot was his own preference. When Shelly joined him, Mike started talking.

"You know, if Danny asked us to go to Disney World, we'd do what we could to take him."

"So we're going to Florida? When did you make this decision?"

"No, no . . . It's Sunday School. He loves it so much, and everything seems to say it's doing him good, and what are we thinking when we drive away right after church service when Danny enjoys something so good?"

"I've been thinking the same thing. If he were into karate and loving it, we'd be driving him to tournaments every other weekend if we had to. Seems to me that Sunday School is a reasonable investment of our time."

Mike nodded.

The tonsillectomy went off without a hitch. Caryn Simms, Danny's Sunday School teacher, heard about Danny's bout with his tonsils and dropped off a get-well card. Sunday afternoon she called Mike and Shelly to let them know that Danny's Sunday School class was praying for him.

Shelly was genuinely moved by Caryn's message on behalf of the class. "And, Miss Simms . . ."

"Please call me Caryn."

"Caryn, thanks so much for your card. Ever since he got it, he's been sleeping with it under his pillow. You know, four year olds don't get that much mail. Except for the cards from his grandparents, yours is the only one he's received. That made his day."

"I'm glad to do it. Danny's a wonderful asset to have in class. I love to have him there."

The conversation turned to casual chitchat after that. Caryn talked about how gratifying it was for her to hear Danny tell about what he'd done at home in response to the last Sunday School session he'd attended. Shelly talked about her surprise that Sunday School gave that kind of "homework"—and what a kick both she and Mike got out of Danny "bringing the lesson home."

"You know, that's one of the most encouraging things I can hear as a Sunday School teacher, Shelly. I love hearing it from him, and I love hearing it from you, too. Please call me anytime you have questions about what we're teaching Danny. You're welcome to sit in on a class, too."

"Really?"

"Absolutely. Especially if you're willing to pitch in during crafts!"

"Thanks for the invitation!"

Of course, there was no way for Caryn to know about the Burnses' decision regarding Danny and Sunday School. So Caryn seemed genuinely surprised when Danny came into class that Sunday with his parents in tow. "Danny kept sleeping with your get-well card under his pillow all week, right through last night." Mike looked around at the classroom and whistled softly. "Wow, has Sunday School changed since I was here!"

"You know what Danny told us this morning?" Shelly picked up the conversation as though she and Caryn were still connected over the phone. "We gave him the option of coming to Sunday School and church today or not. He's much better, but the doctor said not to push him too hard. 'I have to be in Sunday School,' Danny said. 'They need me there.'"

"Hi, Miss Simms! Guess what? I did what we said I should do the last time I was here!" Danny hadn't missed a beat from losing his tonsils.

"Let's get everyone together so we can all hear about it, Danny.

You know something? I'm so glad you're back! We really need you here."

Shelly and Mike looked out of place for an instant, then they sat down with the children in a circle. "Ready for some help with crafts today, Miss Simms?"

Watch This Principle

Let's review this principle: *Like the two wings of an airplane, home and church must be connected in order for a child to soar spiritually.* Let's explain what we mean.

A good Sunday School lesson will begin where a child is, help the child learn and understand biblical truth, and then send the child home with a mission—to apply the lesson truth in concrete ways in the coming week. An alert faith parent will pick up on the lesson focus, help guide application, and take the child even further than the teacher could in a limited class time. By the next Sunday, the child has had the opportunity to make some significant spiritual progress—because home and church were working hand in hand.

Caryn Simms continues to work this principle to the hilt— and Jack and Shelly Burns are learning how to do it too.

You might not expect four year olds to be such prime candidates for a home/church feedback loop, but Danny is for Caryn and the Burns family. Part of their secret is that they keep the connection simple. At church, Caryn sets up the response part of the lesson in a simple activity a four year old can do at home. At home, Mike and Shelly take their cues from Danny's verbal report on class that week and his take-home paper. Then they come up with fun opportunities for Danny to achieve his objective.

Danny goes back to Sunday School week after week with reports of success—and as the adage says, "Success breeds success."

The Burnses and Caryn are all good listeners. This isn't something to take for granted. They honestly enjoy engaging in conversation. Listening is a crucial part of a successful feedback loop. Please don't underestimate its positive benefits in the home/church link.

Home/Church Linking

It's true that you can work to instill godly values in your children without linking up with the Sunday School. But why ask your children to work with two different Bible sequences when reinforcing the same Bible truths will result in more effective learning? We see this as a stewardship issue—making the most of the resources God has given us. And one of our most valuable resources is the Sunday School.

Here are some hints for linking successfully with your faith-development partner:

Review the take-home assignment with your children. Your kids need to see that you think the lesson is important, that you take Sunday School seriously. Spending time to clarify what the home application is and to question your children on their experience will do just that.

Check your child's take-home materials for suggested applications of the Sunday School lesson at home or school. Be aware of ways you can help your child succeed in the application—but don't do it for him.

If you need to, adapt the take-home application from the Sunday School lesson to better fit your child's circumstances. Perhaps you're a home schooler, for example, and the application asks for your child to do something regarding friends at school. Take the time to talk through what your child can do with friends at soccer practice or friends at church that still makes the lesson apply. Significant revisions here sometimes require a delicate balance, especially for students from the middle elementary years and up. You don't want to make the application so simple that it holds no challenge for your child, but you can't afford to make it impossible, either.

If you notice that your child is not responding to home application, talk with him or her about it. Every child will have his or her own take on the importance of home application. You can gently reinforce the application or even revise it. But this step is crucial in helping your child understand that what is learned at Sunday School isn't meant to be trapped inside the church walls: it needs to come alive at home, too.

Look for a variety of ways to reinforce the lesson theme during the week. Use books, videos, games, and anything else you can find to help kids remember and apply the lesson. And look for spontaneous opportunities—teachable moments—to bring up the theme.

Believe it or not, most Sunday School teachers (and kids) would love it if you nurtured a significant connection through the home/church link. Your kids would go to Sunday School with a feeling like Danny's: "They need me here." And starting with the Sunday School lesson can also help you, as a parent, increase the impact of your own teaching activities.

The tools are in your hands already—so make the most of them.

Growing with Your Children 8

FAITH KIDS MATURE AT DIFFERENT RATES and in different ways; we need to accept those differences and patiently trust God for the final outcome.

The first round of shouting stirred Penny from her Sunday afternoon nap. The second round made her sit bolt upright on the couch.

She got up and walked briskly to the patio door. She looked over the fence into her neighbor's backyard. Andrew was at it again! There was a huge water fight going on between her fifteen year old and Brian, their nine-year-old neighbor. Squirt guns with backpacks, the water hose running, and a bucket full of water balloons near the Stevenses' back door told the story. And poor

Bob Stevens, still working through the issues of becoming a single parent just a year after his wife left him. He was still on the prayer list at church. Even though Bob and Brian seemed to have done as well as could be expected after Diane left, he probably needed his rest just as much as Penny did.

Penny made her way to the fence to call Andrew out on the carpet when she noticed the Stevenses' back door open. It was Bob Stevens—carrying another bucket full of water balloons!

Penny's mouth was probably still gaping in shock when Bob looked over and waved. He was grinning as if he didn't have a care in the world. She heard him say, "Boys, I need a time-out while I go talk with Andrew's mom. Keep the water away from the fence! Deal?"

Andrew immediately turned to face his mother. "Mom, are you armed?"

Penny raised her hands. "No. The only weapon I have is to ground you until you leave for college if you get me wet."

Andrew shrugged. "That works." Then he turned his attention back to Brian, who greeted him with a face full of water. The melee began again, but the boys did a reasonable job of keeping it on the other side of the yard.

Bob himself was partially drenched. "Penny, I wanted to let you and Rod know how much Andrew has helped Brian over the past few months."

Penny wasn't sure she'd heard Bob correctly. "Helped Brian?"

"Absolutely. It may not seem like much to him, maybe to you

either, but getting Brian to be rowdy is nearly a miracle."

Penny was confused. "Well, Brian always seemed to be the serious, responsible type."

Bob nodded. "He is. Too much so for a nine year old, in my opinion. In some ways, his taking on responsibility really helps. His room looks much better at his tender age than any of my bachelor apartments ever looked. He tackles his homework as if he's working on a Rhodes scholarship. And it's a lot more that way since Diane left."

"I wish some of his maturity in those areas would rub off on Andrew!"

"Maybe it will. I'm sure happy about the part of Andrew that's rubbing off on Brian."

"Oh, you wouldn't be if you saw his room. And Andrew's study habits are atrocious. He does what he has to just to get by."

"I understand. I had an older brother just like that. He really didn't hit the books until he found something at a college he thought he was interested in. From that point on, he was on the dean's list every semester. Runs his own company now. I was like Brian. Serious, overcommitted; I really forgot how to play. My older brother still calls me now and then to remind me to take a break. You know, my parents always called me 'the mature one' and wondered whether my brother would ever grow up. We both ended up all right—just matured in different areas at different rates.

"But the reason I'm at the fence is to let you know that having Andrew come around every once in a while to play ball or to have a water fight is really a blessing. I don't know how many other fifteen year olds would give a nine year old a second look, much less get down and play with them for a while. And these times with Andrew are some of the few times I see Brian actually kick back and relax—he's not the 'little man' anymore, he's a kid again. Just let Andrew know sometime soon how much I appreciate it, will you? I'll tell him myself—but it might be tough for Andrew to believe me while I'm throwing water balloons at him at point blank range, you know?"

Watch This Principle

Here's another look at the principle of this chapter: *Faith kids mature at different rates and in different ways; we need to accept those differences and patiently trust God for the final outcome.*

Most parents have had to apply this truth of "unique maturation" simply by virtue of being parents. After all, no two kids—even those of the same age—show the same maturity in every area of life.

One thing we parents tend to forget about maturation: we're still maturing, too. So the big point for us to recognize is that each person in our family—adult and child alike—matures in a unique way.

In our story, Bob faced a challenge as a father. He knew that Brian was finding ways to cope with his family situation, but Bob wanted to give his son some other options—options that Bob himself hadn't taken advantage of at Brian's age. Seeing the similarities between Andrew and his own brother gave him an idea. He saw the differences between Andrew and Brian as something positive—and put them together in ways that would benefit both of them.

Everyone has a different maturation pattern. This truth is important to you as a faith parent. God brings people, including the people in your family, to points of maturity in different ways.

How will this principle work out with your own children? We don't know. For instance, take the issue of personal responsibility. Some teenagers still have to learn a work ethic, while some nine year olds are eager-beaver entrepreneurs. That isn't to say that they all won't mature into fine adult workers—it's just that their points of maturation differ.

This leads to another point of the principle that most parents learn to appreciate: maturation involves more than head knowledge. It encompasses every aspect of a person's life development. Sometimes experience is the necessary factor in bringing about maturity in a given area. For instance, look at the things that await your children in the future: higher education, career, marriage, and parenthood are just a few areas that come to mind.

Your children will have some ideas on these subjects when they're still very young, but it's their real-life experiences that will bring about the maturation of those ideas.

Home/Church Linking

So how can you make the most of this maturation principle in the home/church link?

As much as possible, trust God's timing in bringing appropriate maturation to each of your children. We know from experience that we sometimes have to call for greater maturity from our children. At the same time, we try to set realistic expectations according to development. (You can find out more about those expectations in the next section of this book, beginning with chapter 12.) God's timing is good, and He can be trusted.

Realize that even children in the same family will mature at their own paces. It's only natural for parents to compare one child with another—after all, we want all our children to be the best they can be. But we also know how hurtful the "Why can't you be like Johnny" remarks can be. We don't want to damage a child's confidence in his or her own value. How can we use the differences between children to actually encourage them? How can we use those differences as a way of appreciating God's creativity and the value of each unique individual? We think it's worth the effort.

Remember that maturation involves not only physical growth, but spiritual development as well. Some children seem compliant and accepting of spiritual truth; others seem to wrestle with God for years, as Jacob did. We can help our children realize that in all the upheavals of life, the one constant is our unchanging God, who never gives up on His children.

Patience is a virtue that needs to be put into practice by the parent, the teacher, and the child alike. Watching for maturity in a child is like watching water boil: if you wait and watch second-by-second for the results, you might believe they'll never happen.

Faith kids need to know that God values them just as they are—and also that He wants them to develop into all they can become. You can reinforce the home/church link by applying the truth that maturity is an issue that God works out on a person-by-person basis—and that you love each of your kids wherever they are in the maturity process. And what will really convince them of this truth is their seeing you continue to mature in Christ.

Model Your Faith 9

FAITH PARENTS DON'T JUST TALK ABOUT GOD—they show their children what God is like.

"Mom, can Sara come home with me Friday and spend the night?"

"What's our rule about that?"

"We have the parents talk about it."

I hope that rule sticks when Cheri's sixteen. Jane sighed and thanked God that was still ten years away. "Do you have Sara's phone number so I can talk with one of her parents?"

"Here it is."

"Cheri, did you remember that Friday is family night? Do you think that'll be okay with Sara?"

"I think so."

Jane dialed the number. Cheri had written one six backwards, but the number was still legible. A voice on the other end answered.

"Hello?"

"Hello. I'm Jane Mullins. My daughter Cheri attends school with Sara."

"Oh, Cheri's mom? Sara talks about Cheri all the time. They seem to have hit it off very well."

"Cheri seems pretty taken with Sara, too. We'd like to ask Sara to spend the night this Friday, if that works out with your schedule. And so you have a face to attach to the voice, I'd like to meet with you before then if you have the time."

"What if we took the girls to Burger Clown after school tomorrow? They could use the play park while we talk."

"Great idea! See you there."

Jane Mullins and Ruth Lavin hit it off almost as well as their daughters did. And Jane was encouraged when she broached the subject of Sara being a part of the Mullins family night.

"Ruth, I want you to know that Fridays are our family nights. We usually order pizza, play some board games, and then we have a short time where we do an activity that helps us tell a story or principle from the Bible. Then we pray. We would never force a guest to join us, but that's so much of our Friday night routine that I wouldn't want Sara to be uncomfortable whether or not you wanted her to join in."

Ruth smiled. "That's not a problem at all. In fact, let me tell you something that sold me on Sara becoming friends with Cheri. The very first day of school, Sara fell and scraped her knee. Cheri came over to help. She said to Sara, 'Look, I'm gonna hug you now while I pray for your knee to feel better. That's what my mom does for me, and it always works.'

"It worked for Sara, too. She came home and told me about it that night. I figured right then that if a six year old knew enough to hug and pray as first responses to a problem, she must have seen it at home—and we needed to become family friends."

Watch This Principle

It bears repeating: *Faith parents don't just talk about God—they show their children what God is like.*

There are very few issues as crucial as this one to the faith parent. You've heard the saying before: what is caught is usually more important than what is taught.

The inborn assumption of a child is that Mom and Dad are as

close to God as anyone else they know. In fact, for the first few years of life Mom and Dad are nearly objects of worship to their kids. (This is probably only a fond memory for those of you now dealing with adolescents who are convinced you left your brains in San Francisco.) It's no myth that many of our own ideas about God are initially based on how we perceived and how we related to our parents.

We mention this principle not to instill fear or guilt in you, but to encourage you to simply face the fact that you are showing God to your children. It doesn't matter whether we like the idea. We can't avoid this responsibility. To our young children, God is like us. So how are we doing as a voice for God's Word and a model of His ways for the children He has given us?

Being your child's first example of God's ways is crucial to your children's spiritual development. If teaching by word alone is all a child experiences at home, that child may conclude that the Word is either impossible to live out or completely irrelevant to everyday life. Otherwise, someone in the family would be demonstrating how to live God's Word, right? If teaching by model alone is all that happens at home, the child might conclude that Christianity has no real object of faith (such as Jesus Christ) and is only a set of lifestyle principles stated slightly differently than those of, say, scouting.

Your first response might be something like "It's not fair! No human being can represent God perfectly." You're right. It is impossible. But it's still a fact that our children look at us that way. However, the good news is that we don't have to act in spectacular, artificial ways. Remember how Cheri copied her mother's pattern when Sara scraped her knee? We can begin in small ways.

And God doesn't expect us to do it alone. He has provided the Holy Spirit—and other people—to help.

Home/Church Linking

Here are a few hints to help you be an effective model for your children—in partnership with your teammates at church:

Remember that you are called to be both a human voice for God's Word and a human model of God's ways as a parent. Your job is to transmit values and principles, to be sure. Your stories and words will make a difference. But your actions and attitudes in everyday life will likely be even more memorable to your children as they make their own decisions about whether or not to be disciples of Jesus Christ.

Rely on God. God doesn't expect you to take on this responsibility alone. He has promised never to leave us or forsake us. He has promised to strengthen us and guide us. Since we can't do this in our own strength, we must depend on Him. Be openly dependent on God. Let your children observe your own attitude toward God. Be willing to admit your failures, ask your children's forgiveness when necessary, and then let them see your determination—by God's grace—to do it better next time.

Your children will never outgrow this need. As they get older and begin to wrestle with ethical and theological issues, make the theoretical principles human. Your hugging them, listening to them, or praying with them will add a personal dimension that "God talk" just can't achieve. Modeling God's ways can be as simple as that—but it is crucially important.

Suggest ways that your children can become models for others. This can happen through the home application of a Sunday School lesson or by encouraging them to take on roles that put them in these positions. For instance, your older children might be able to take on volunteer teaching roles for the church. They could "adopt" a lonely senior citizen as a "grandparent" and visit while they do some household chores for him or her.

Make no mistake: your modeling is the litmus test that your children will use to evaluate both you and God. Most importantly, this principle reminds us that, as parents, we are often "the first Jesus" our children see and hear. So let's pray that God will give us the ability to represent Him faithfully—and give our children the grace to see God as He is, in spite of our imperfect examples.

Supply multiple models for your children. Their Sunday School teachers, other church leaders, and your Christian friends can all contribute to this role. Because in the long run, we don't want our children to copy everything about us. We want them to imitate the Christlike character they see—in us and in a variety of mature Christians.

A final note on the humanity principle: Are you reluctant to trust your life completely to God because of your own childhood experiences? Perhaps a Christian counselor is the right first step

Model Your Faith

for you. Then take the risk of joining a group of God's people. It won't be easy, especially if you've tried it before and been hurt. And even the most sensitive group will make mistakes. Even after you've made such a commitment, healing takes time. But the remarkable truth is that God does work through His people—imperfect though they be. In relationship with your spiritual brothers and sisters, you can come to know your Heavenly Father in a life-changing way.

Be
Encouraging

10

Faith development is a lifelong process; we all need encouragement to keep going.

Louella and Deke Johnson were blessed with not one, but two, later-in-life surprises. As a result, life in the city was busier than ever. Deke held both a full-time and a part-time job so Louella could be home with Daniel and Douglas. They kept going to church every Sunday and brought the boys with them from the first Sunday after each of them came home from the maternity ward.

The boys were stair steps, now in the fourth and fifth grades. Daniel was maybe an inch taller than his younger brother, but Douglas had a more stocky build and likely outweighed Daniel by ten pounds.

Daniel and Douglas were in Jim Hope's fourth and fifth grade Sunday School class. Deke and Louella took special pride in the fact that their boys lived out what they learned in "Mr. Jim's" class—and from the family times they shared together.

One evening, Deke roused himself from his favorite chair in the living room to get Louella from the kitchen. "Lou, look at this!" He motioned to the boys, who were planted in front of the TV.

The show was about kids who were running drugs for a gang. Daniel was livid with what he saw. "No way! No way should they be doing that! Don't they know they're helping those guys hurt other people?"

Deke was obviously proud of Daniel. "I like the way our boy thinks, don't you?"

Then Douglas, quite involved in the show, delivered the punch line: "Bet they didn't pay attention in Sunday School."

Louella smiled. "We should have Mr. Jim over for Sunday dinner soon. He's really getting through to the boys."

A lot was "getting through" to the boys from both church and home. Daniel and Douglas enjoyed a simple faith that was completely in line with the "right and wrong" emphasis of their developmental stage. In fact, they sometimes functioned as the class policemen at Sunday School and at their elementary school.

And another time . . . well, Daniel and Douglas came home escorted by the pastor and a policeman. Louella's heart sank when she saw the sight at the door. "Oh, what happened? Are you in trouble? Do you know what your father will do when he gets home and hears about this?"

"I hope Deke will be proud of both your boys, Louella." Pastor Ricketts was grinning from ear to ear.

"That's right, Mrs. Johnson." The policeman nodded in agreement.

"Then what's this about?"

"Well, Mom, you know how Daniel and I like to play one-on-one basketball over on the church lot?" Douglas didn't wait for her to answer. "Just a few minutes ago, I blew by Daniel for a layup, and he was just standing there. He never just stands there, so I checked him out and he was staring at the church basement windows. So I looked over there, and… "

"Mom, there was Chuckie Freeman crawling into the church kitchen window. Of course, I didn't know it was Chuckie Freeman right away. So we saw Pastor's car still in his parking space, and we ran to his office to warn him about someone in the kitchen."

"So Pastor calls the

police, and Officer Jenkins here comes over with a silent siren—
that means lights but no sound, Mom—and we wait upstairs
while he and Pastor go downstairs to check the kitchen . . ."

"And they find Chuckie Freeman right when he's trying to
push a microwave out the window! He'd filled the microwave
with food and stuff from the church pantry . . ."

"Do you think he was hungry?" Douglas was trying to sort out
what might have led Chuckie to such a bad choice and was trying
to give him the benefit of the doubt.

"Anyway, Chuckie was busted on the spot, and I know him
from school, so while Pastor and Officer Jenkins called his
parents, I came up with this great idea: why not have Chuckie
some to Sunday School with us? So I said, 'We need to put this
guy in our Sunday School class.'"

Douglas followed up. "Then I said, 'Yeah, then he'd learn to
do the right thing.' And guess what? Chuckie's parents, the pastor,
and Officer Jenkins thought it was a great idea too!"

Louella hugged her sons. "I am so proud of you two. And your
father will be so happy to hear this about our two favorite boys!"

Pastor Ricketts nodded. "These boys of yours, Louella—
they're always thinking."

"They get that from their father."

About a half hour later, the phone rang. It was Jim Hope.
"Mrs. Johnson, I just heard about the boys stopping the burglary
at the church. I wanted to call you and tell you how much I
appreciate them both."

"Oh, they talk about you all the time. They're always saying something about Sunday School."

"Could I talk to one of them?"

"If you like, talk to them both. I'll let one of them use the extension in my bedroom."

"That would be great, Mrs. Johnson."

Seconds later, the boys were pouring out their version of the story over the phone for Jim's benefit. "Guys, you were great. Thanks for watching out for the church that way. Hey, your mom tells me you're always talking about Sunday School when you're at home. She says you're really good about doing the home assignment part of the lesson. So why don't I ever hear about that the next Sunday?"

Douglas talked first. "You know, Mr. Jim, Daniel and I decided a while back . . ."

And Daniel continued, " . . . that we talked so much during the rest of class that we'd let the other kids cover the first ten minutes. That okay with you?"

Watch This Principle

Here is the principle of encouragement again: *Faith development is a lifelong process; we all need encouragement to keep going.*

There's no way to force enthusiasm into faith kids like Daniel and Douglas.

Daniel and Douglas are blessed with parents who encourage them. Mrs. Johnson is vocal with her praise of them, and she's not afraid to brag on her boys to others even when the boys are close enough to overhear. These two have received so much praise for doing the right thing when they've made good choices that they want to do what's right. "Bringing Sunday School home" has become one of the "right things" they do. So has exercising the same respect for Mr. Jim as they have for their parents.

Jim completes the encouragement loop in his role as the boys' Sunday School teacher. As in this instance, Jim calls his students and their parents at home with words of support and affirmation when something special happens.

It's a lot easier for a child to succeed in taking the lessons of faith wherever he goes with such a supportive network.

Home/Church Linking

So how can you make the most of this principle in your own home/church link?

Be a lavish encourager. More than prizes or treats, simple encouragement is still the best motivator for children. Sure, rewards are fine once in a while, but they're not essential. Rewards without vocal encouragement from you ring hollow; sincere encouragement has a bigger payoff than a hundred candy bars.

Help your children make connections between the Bible and everyday life. Whether it's a situation that demonstrates the difference between right and wrong or a question about how to act when a friend makes fun of you, the Bible has insights for your children about everyday life. You can help them find the connection

Be Encouraging

and then encourage them as they put Bible truths into practice.

Encourage your kids to think through their own ideas about transferring faith principles they've learned to everyday life. Offer examples from your own life. After reading a story together, ask a question like "How do you think you could apply the principle from this story at home? At school?"

The reason Daniel and Douglas are so good at making connections between Sunday School and home—and back again—is that they've been coached to do just that for years. Encouragement isn't a one-time quick fix. But over time, as you nurture your children's faith, you'll begin to see biblical values taking root in their lives. That's one of the most gratifying experiences in faith parenting.

How Does It Fit?

11

W HAT WE TEACH, AND HOW WE TEACH IT, should change as the child develops.

Mark Hunt was desperately hoping for some divine insight. His third grader, Jake, had seemed really restless during the last few rounds of family devotions. Mark had never seen that kind of behavior in Jake before. *Maybe it's just a phase,* Mark thought hopefully. *On the other hand, maybe I should get to the bottom of this now.*

As they sat down around the den for devotions, Mark took the proverbial bull by the horns. "So, Jake, I've noticed you haven't really seemed to get much out of devotions lately. Is there something we need to talk about?"

There was no hesitation in Jake's response. He pointed to the children's Bible, dog-eared from years of use, that Mark held in his hands. "Dad, do I have to listen to the Bible story from this book?"

Mark was surprised at how strongly his son had stated his case. "Well, Buddy, I guess I need some help understanding what the problem is. You've loved hearing Bible stories from this book since you were three. I don't understand what the problem is now."

Jake shook his head. "Dad, that's the point! The Bible book we use is for *babies*. I need to use the real thing now!" He held up the Bible he'd received at Sunday School as he entered the third grade.

Mark was surprised at how he felt. He was shaken a bit, in fact. He hadn't really anticipated a need to move out of the children's Bible for a few more years. But then he thought about it: could he realistically expect Jake to stay in tune with family devotions if he thought the content was just "for babies" ?

Mark cleared his throat. "Fair enough, Sport. I guess I really wasn't thinking about the fact that you've moved into a new level of Bible study. We'll have to change some things, won't we?"

Jake smiled in satisfaction. "Thanks, Dad. But hey, if you really need to, we can still use our old Bible every once in awhile."

And at that moment Mark realized that if they occasionally used the "old Bible," it probably would be because *he* needed to— not because Jake needed it.

Mark said, "So, Jake, take a look in your Bible at Ecclesiastes 3. That's in the Old Testament. Tonight we'll read about how God has everything set up to happen in its own time...."

Watch This Principle

Here's the principle again: *What we teach, and how we teach it, should change as the child develops.*

In this story, the main focus is on Jake's declaration about the children's Bible story book. But we need to give just as much emphasis to Mark. He had fostered an environment in which Jake could speak his mind freely. And he was sensitive enough to his son's needs to change his own practices.

As a faith parent, you'll find a lot of examples of this principle in action. If you're communicating about faith and it seems too complex to a young child, he or she will tune you out. So will the teenager who doesn't hear from you that faith can be applied to more complex issues, too.

Let's illustrate with examples from the life of David. Many Bible story books tell about David's experiences as the poet-shepherd, and rightly so. Those stories are attractive to and can be understood by even young children. But David's life story goes far beyond his shepherd years, which are addressed in relatively few chapters of the Bible. Many more chapters are devoted to his life as a warrior and a king. Those chapters contain accounts of David's failures, including adultery and murder. As children mature into teenagers and young adults, they need to be exposed to the full witness of David's life—especially those parts that they'd have had difficulty understanding as children.

As you teach God's Word and model His ways to your children, try not to limit yourself to those "fits all ages" parts of the

Bible. Keep your children's developmental level in mind. That way, God's Word can touch them in just the right ways for their ages, whether they're preschoolers or teenagers. Once in a while, you can still have common family faith lessons using portions of Scripture that all can understand. Just be sure to take opportunities for one-on-one time with each of your children to address them at their level of development.

Home/Church Linking

Use these hints for making the principle of making children's lessons fit their developmental level work in the home/church link:

When looking at your children's development, consider other things besides age. You might evaluate your children's books, videos, family devotions book, or other resources by asking questions such as these: Is the reading level appropriate for their ages? Are the issues relevant to their lives? Will the principles help them grow in faith?

Reshape the activity ideas you find—or the stories you tell—that don't fit your children well. Most parents do this instinctively. Just remember that the goal of faith parenting is to allow God's Word to have maximum impact on your children, not to follow a written lesson or activity to the letter.

Periodically ask your children if the approach you're using helps them understand God and the Bible better. Your children are the best reflectors on your faith parenting approach, bar none. Although you likely won't meet their every desire in your efforts to help them grow in the faith, sometimes their comments can help you discover better ways to connect effectively with them. So listen.

Faith parents must consider the development levels of their children if they are to succeed. You may be wondering, "Just how do I do that?"

That's why we're here. The next section of this book will give you a concise and concrete guide to strategies you can use now to succeed at home with almost every age and stage of development in your efforts to grow faith kids.

Toddlers and Two Year Olds

12

"GOOD MORNING, JEREMY!" Melissa, the teacher of toddlers, knelt down and held out her arms. Two-year-old Jeremy ran toward her for a quick hug, then bounced over to his favorite activity center. As Jeremy began piling blocks into the semblance of a wall, Melissa stood and greeted the parents. "Thanks for bringing Jeremy again!"

"He wouldn't let us miss it, even if we wanted to," laughed Mark. "This is one of the highlights of his week."

"I'm glad he feels that way," said Melissa. "And I really appreciate your help, too. Jeremy's really learning a lot."

"How do you know how much he's learning?" asked Kathy. "He seems to forget things quickly, even if we go over the rhymes and songs with him every day."

"That repetition is one of the most important things you can do," Melissa assured them. "Coming here every week makes this classroom feel familiar and safe. He's learning that he can trust me and the teaching assistants. Hearing and doing the same things over and over also makes him feel comfortable and safe. As he hears about God in this safe situation, he'll begin to think of God as Someone he can trust. And as he hears the same things at home, that will further strengthen his feeling that he can trust himself to God."

"So you're saying that what he's 'learning' isn't just information. He's learning attitudes about us, about you, about church, and these attitudes lay the foundation for his attitudes toward God."

"That's right." Melissa smiled. "Again, thanks for your help. We've got to work together in order to do this right!"

For two year olds, that's what a successful home/church link looks like. The number one agenda is building trust. What we say to these young children, how we say it, how we treat them, the way we repeat things till they become familiar, the predictable environment we set up for them—all these combine to help the children feel safe and protected. And as they learn to trust us—both parents and teachers—they will be more open to trusting God later on.

Toddlers and Two Year Olds

HOW TODDLERS AND TWO YEAR OLDS LEARN

Two year olds are:

- imitators
- experimenters
- learning language skills
- learning through important relationships—
  especially with their parents
- self-contained (they learn better as individuals than in groups)

TODDLERS AND TWOS:
WHAT WORKS, WHAT DOESN'T

DO

- ✔ Create a safe, interesting home environment where your child can freely explore.
- ✔ In your everyday talking, refer frequently to God, Jesus, and the Bible to lay a solid foundation for future spiritual teaching.
- ✔ Tell Bible stories briefly, using movement and participation.
- ✔ Encourage lots of talking and repeating.
- ✔ Connect with your child's Sunday School teacher.
- ✔ Use crafts and art projects that allow your toddler to enjoy being creative.

DON'T

- ✘ Don't have any unsafe conditions that keep children from moving about safely.
- ✘ Don't assume that your toddler is too young to be exposed to Bible truths.

✘ Don't tell lengthy Bible stories as your child sits passively.

✘ Don't discourage your toddler from interrupting your story-telling; that interaction is very important to his understanding.

✘ Don't be satisfied with crafts that require coloring within the lines or in which there's only one way to do it right.

Preschoolers (3–5 Years)

13

"MOMMA, WHY IS GOD A BIRD?"

Tess wasn't quite sure she'd heard her four-year-old daughter, Lori, correctly. "Could you say your question again, please?"

"Why is God a bird?"

"Honey, God isn't a bird."

"Miss Steffi said the same thing. But that's what she said in Sunday School today."

This was going to be a great story. Tess settled Lori on her knee. "So what did you hear Miss Steffi say this morning?"

"Well, we learned about the Holy Parrot."

"The Holy Parrot?"

"Yeah. You know the story where the bird comes down from heaven over Jesus? Miss Steffi first said it was like a dove, but then she called it 'the Holy Parrot.' If God's a parrot, that means He's my favorite bird! Like the one in the pet store window!"

"Well, Honey, I think Miss Steffi might have said 'Holy Spirit' instead of 'Holy Parrot.' At least that's how I remember the story."

"So God's a ghost and not a bird?"

"Not exactly. Tell you what. Let's get your Bible storybook and read about this again. Why don't you go get it while I make a phone call?"

Tess was in pretty constant communication with Steffi about Lori's Christian education. That afternoon, Tess called Steffi laughing.

"Guess what question Lori asked me today?"

"The same one she asked at the end of class: why is God a bird?"

"Ah, she asked you the same question! Well, I had to follow up on that. I asked her what she learned in Sunday School this morning. She said, 'I learned about the Holy Parrot.'"

"The Holy Parrot?"

"You know, Steffi, she heard you talk about the dove coming down from heaven and the Holy Spirit. Her mind made the jump from that conversation to her favorite bird at the pet shop: that pretty parrot in the front window. The result was the 'Holy Parrot.'"

"Tell you what. I'll review this lesson next Sunday just to make sure we don't have pet shop deities in the minds of any other kids. Is Lori still wondering why God is a bird?"

"We're still working on that. I think that review could really help."

Sometimes building faith kids means keeping the content responsive to their needs.

HOW PRESCHOOLERS LEARN

Preschoolers' brains are hungry for input from a variety of sources. That's why they love the question "Why?" so much. Preschoolers are:

- questioners
- able to focus on only one aspect of a situation at a time
- sensory learners (they learn well through activity)
- able to do many more things physically than toddlers and twos
- group learners (they can participate in family faith discussions)
- roaming learners

TEACHING DOS AND DON'TS FOR PRESCHOOLERS

DO

✔ Tell Bible stories with the Bible open at the appropriate passage to reinforce the fact that the stories come from the Bible and that they are true.

✔ Provide activities that allow your preschooler to use large-muscle skills.

✔ Offer a variety of activities that use as many of the senses as possible.

✔ Provide opportunities for your child to practice his developing finger dexterity skills such as cutting, coloring, sorting, and stringing.

✔ Encourage creative play experiences: dramatization, music, playacting, and movement.

✔ Allow your child's expanding vocabulary to be stretched through verbal interaction.

✔ Encourage his natural curiosity by valuing his questions.

DON'T

✘ Don't concentrate so much on making the Bible stories entertaining that your child misses the point that the stories come from the Bible, which came from God.

✘ Don't expect your preschooler to sit quietly for long periods of time.

✘ Don't give your child craft activities in which an adult has done most of the work and the child merely does the assembly.

✘ Don't expect preschool children to be the audience and not the participants.

✘ Don't do all the talking.

✘ Don't discourage or ignore the constant "whys" you will hear.

Early Elementary Children

14

"Okay. Daddy, are you ready?"

"Yes. I want to fight that silly shepherd boy and make his people my slaves!" Dan walked out from the hallway, growling and brandishing a broomstick in one hand and a trash can lid in the other. "Where is that shrimp?"

"Now, Julia, do your Philistine cheer."

"Go, Goliath! Ah-hah! Go, Goliath!" At eleven, Julia was definitely looking forward to middle school cheerleading tryouts.

"Joe? The announcer, please."

"Ladies and gentlemen: On this side of the valley, coming in at nine cubits and weighing about the same as a small county, give it up for GOLIATH!"

The family made sound effects while Dan did a stage bow.

"And on this side of the valley, short but brave, skinny but faithful, the Kid Shepherd: DAVID!"

More sound effects. "Now, LET'S get READY to RUMBLE!" If you gave Joe the right role, he still loved these family skits at the age of fourteen.

"Okay, Justin. Remember your line?"

"Sure do, Mom. But Dad has one first."

"Oh, that's right! Here we go: Hey, Israel! Who do you think I am, that you send a child like this to fight me?"

"Cool, Dad! My turn: You look big, Goliath, but my God is a lot bigger. The battle is His!" Then six-year-old Justin waved a foam ball around his head three times, let it loose and pegged Dan squarely in the forehead.

For early elementary students, simple dramas like this are one of the best faith lessons that can be offered. But given the dramatic fall Dan took to the living room floor, our opinion is that dads like them at least as much.

HOW EARLY ELEMENTARY CHILDREN LEARN

Early elementary students are:

- dramatists and role-players
- hands-on creators
- simple, focused, concrete thinkers
- almost consumed by the process of learning to read

Early Elementary Children

DOS AND DON'TS FOR EARLY ELEMENTARY CHILDREN

DO

✔ Establish eye contact with the child and smile when talking with him.

✔ Provide reading material appropriate for your child's reading abilities.

✔ Encourage your child to show that he knows exactly what the Bible story is about by retelling the Bible content using dramatization, puppets, or role-playing.

✔ Promote interactive creativity by providing activity choices that include cutting, constructing, and creating.

✔ Use books and activities that match the learning of your new reader—recognizing letters, frequent writing opportunities, repetitive text to read.

✔ Recognize that the most important book your child will ever be exposed to is the Bible.

DON'T

✘ Don't underestimate what a child will pick up from your facial expressions.

✘ Don't expect a new reader to be able to read complex material.

✘ Don't assume your child has understood the Bible content simply because the story is finished.

✘ Don't ignore the fact that learning to read is a consuming part of your child's life.

✘ Don't miss opportunities to relate your child's new reading abilities to a future of reading the Bible.

Elementary Children 15

 EIGHT-YEAR-OLD CHRISTOPHER WAS A REALITY TESTER. Every idea that came up during family faith activities—or Sunday School, for that matter—was put under scrutiny.

"That doesn't sound right." That simple statement would send the Hill family off on a discussion about what was real and what wasn't, what was true and what was false, what was right and what was wrong.

Christopher's mother, Linda, wondered whether Christopher was actually questioning the faith or just questioning to learn. She voiced her concern to her husband, Ralph. They agreed to watch Christopher for indications of how his faith was doing.

A few days later, Ralph stuck his head around the corner as Linda was working on a craft. "Come out to the family room and see this. It's a TV program about a cult. Watch Christopher."

As the show continued and the cult made its arguments about its understanding of God, Christopher kept saying, 'That doesn't sound right. That isn't true. That's not true.'"

Ralph finally asked, "Christopher, how do you know what they believe and do isn't true?"

With all the solemnity an eight year old can muster, Christopher replied, "Dad, when you've been in Sunday School as many years as I have, you know what's right and what's wrong."

Ralph smiled at Linda. "You know, he's in a stage of testing everything these days."

"I'm just glad he's testing what he hears on TV, too." Linda felt a wave of relief. "Let's make sure one of us tells Janice what he said about Sunday School, too."

Faith kids need standards to "test the waters" of what they hear in everyday life. The elementary school age is a prime age developmentally to encourage that kind of testing.

HOW ELEMENTARY CHILDREN LEARN

Elementary children (here, second and third graders) share these characteristics:

- logical thinking
- a love for facts
- demonstrated reasoning and sorting skills
- a sense of "right and wrong" justice
- cooperation with common group goals

TEACHING DOS AND DON'T FOR ELEMENTARY CHILDREN

DO

- ✔ Provide as much factual and background information as you can when presenting a Bible story.
- ✔ Encourage your child to use the Bible to find verses and references.
- ✔ Allow your child to make choices between activities.
- ✔ Work hard to catch your child being good and make a big deal of it.
- ✔ Enjoy your child's corny jokes and puns.

DON'T

- ✘ Don't present Bible stories without giving some sort of context for the stories.
- ✘ Don't tell your children Bible stories without allowing them the chance to look up verses themselves.
- ✘ Don't focus simply on your child's bad or annoying behavior.
- ✘ Don't expect sophisticated humor or adult thinking.

Upper Elementary Children 16

OWEN AND CAROL BARFIELD LOOKED AT EACH OTHER a bit apprehensively as they left Martin at the fourth and fifth grade Sunday School class. Mrs. Tennant, the teacher, seemed very friendly. But they knew the kids in the class could make or break Martin's adjustment to their new hometown.

"I just keep thinking back to when I moved in fifth grade." Carol shook her head as they followed the signs to the adult class. "The kids in my new school treated me like I came straight from the circus train."

"The same kids you cried about leaving at your last class reunion?" Owen chuckled for a moment, then sobered. "There's a big group mentality at that age. I hope things go well for Martin this morning."

You can imagine the Barfields' relief when Martin met them in the church foyer with another boy his age. "Hey, Mom! Dad! This is Stuart. Stuart and the other guys in the class play soccer some Sunday afternoons. When they found out I was a goalie, they asked if I could come play later today. Is that all right with you?"

It was an answered prayer. "Absolutely. Stuart, can we meet your parents and get directions to wherever it is you're playing?" Stuart took the Barfields to a couple across the foyer.

"Mom, Dad, this is Martin! He can play goalie! He's here with his family today. Here are his parents! They're all new in town, and they're at our church!"

Faith kids can bond together and form strong groups. At this age, those groups can become almost exclusionary of others. But it doesn't take much for faith kids to reach outside their group when they're encouraged to do so.

HOW UPPER ELEMENTARY STUDENTS LEARN

These characteristics describe your upper elementary (here, fourth and fifth grade) students:

- an emphasis on group membership
- better analysis of facts and intentions
- logical thinking
- a love for facts
- demonstrated logic and sorting skills
- a strong sense of "right and wrong" justice
- cooperation with common group goals

TEACHING DOS AND DON'TS FOR
UPPER ELEMENTARY CHILDREN

DO

✔ Provide opportunities for your child to study the Bible and look up verses, references, and passages.

✔ Encourage acceptance of all God's children, starting with yours.

✔ Encourage your child to bring friends to visit.

✔ Allow your child to make choices between activities.

✔ Keep family faith activities and lessons as concrete and experiential as possible.

DON'T

✗ Don't simply tell your child the whole family faith lesson as he or she passively listens.

✗ Don't minimize the importance of friends for your child.

Middle Schoolers

T ONY LOOKED OVER at his about-to-be-seventh-grade son. Tim's voice was cracking on a regular basis now—and as Tony looked over at him in the passenger's seat, he noticed a new line of peach fuzz on his upper lip.

"Dad, do you know what I didn't like about sixth grade?"

"Tell me."

"It took me way too long to feel good about switching rooms every class period. And the girls got bigger than me. And we were the pond scum of the whole school."

"So maybe you won't treat this year's sixth graders like pond scum, right?"

Tim grinned. "Right. So you know what I like about seventh grade already? I'm starting out three inches taller, twelve pounds heavier, and the girls look better this year than they did last year."

"This from the boy who said time and again that girls were completely off their rockers just a few months ago?" *Wow, is this change happening fast!*

Faith kids need to learn how to deal with change—and they seem be especially aware of the rate of change in the middle school years. Faith parenting of a child this age is a real adventure!

HOW MIDDLE SCHOOLERS LEARN

Change is the definitive word for sixth, seventh, and eighth grade middle schoolers, who share these characteristics:

- dealing with change in school buildings, routines, and friends
- a profound emphasis on peer relationships
- physical changes (both visible and internal)
- a gradual shift from concrete to abstract thinking
- the ability to reflect on one's own thoughts and actions

TEACHING DOS AND DON'TS FOR
MIDDLE SCHOOLERS

<u>DO</u>

- ✔ Create an atmosphere where every child is valued and included—encourage your child to bring friends home.
- ✔ Expect a lot of energy and physical activity.
- ✔ Encourage the exchange of ideas and much discussion— find out what your middle schooler is thinking.

✔ Pose challenging questions that expand your middle schooler's thinking.

✔ Help your middle schooler understand the symbolism and truths represented in proverbs and parables.

✔ Encourage middle schoolers to consciously apply what they learn from their faith lessons—whether they learn them at home or at church.

DON'T

✘ Don't embarrass your middle schooler in front of friends.

✘ Don't expect your middle schooler to be a passive learner.

✘ Don't do all the talking and expect your middle schooler to listen.

✘ Don't give your middle schooler all the answers; challenge him to independent thought.

✘ Don't expect your middle schooler to fully understand figurative language.

✘ Don't dictate to your middle schooler how to apply faith lessons to his life; to be effective, the application must come from him.

High Schoolers

RACHEL FOUND VALERIE LOOKING AT the backyard from the patio.

"Are you all right, Val?"

"Oh. Hi, Mom. I'm fine. It was just one of those days at school."

"How so?"

"You know, it's hard to be friends with so many different people. I talk with everyone. I get along with the jocks, the brains, the preppies, and the ravers. I really like my friends who are Christian, of course. That's how everyone looks at me."

"Is that a problem?"

"No, that's great. But when I play volleyball, I'm supposed to be a jock. When I go to National Honor Society, I'm a brain.

When I'm at Bible study, I'm a Christian. And when I'm a Christian, I know I need to reach out to everyone.

"Today I just felt like I was getting lost in the shuffle."

Rachel hugged her daughter for a moment. "It happens. Stay strong."

Faith kids in high school are seeking an identity. If you offer strong and compelling faith parenting, you can have a significant impact on their search—and earn the lasting gratitude of your home/church partners—their Sunday School teachers—in the process.

HOW HIGH SCHOOLERS LEARN

These characteristics mark the lives of ninth, tenth, eleventh, and twelfth graders:

- the search for, and establishment of, personal identity
- the profound influence of peers
- the continued shift toward abstract thinking

These characteristics reflect a maturing process that enables a search for values.

TEACHING DOS AND DON'TS FOR
HIGH SCHOOLERS

DO

✔ Expect your high schooler to challenge values and beliefs. Make your home a place where questioning is safe.

✔ Encourage discussion one-on-one among your family members.

✔ Challenge your high schooler to discover what is important to him or her.

✔ Encourage the exchange of ideas and much discussion—find out what your high schooler is thinking.

✔ Expose your high schooler to moral reasoning and biblical values.

✔ Encourage your high schooler to make a plan to apply faith lessons to his or her life.

✔ Be a powerful, positive role model.

DON'T

✘ Don't discourage "big" questions.

✘ Don't assume your high schooler knows what is important.

✘ Don't expect your high schooler to be a passive listener.

✘ Don't do all the talking and expect your high schooler to only listen.

✘ Don't give your high schooler all the answers.

✘ Don't hesitate to challenge your high schooler to think about his or her own moral beliefs.

✘ Don't dictate to your high schooler how to use what he or she has learned.

✘ Don't underestimate the impact you're having on your high schooler.

Adults 19

GENE WAS READY TO COCOON.

He wanted time to himself. He was ready to fall asleep to one of those boring news analysis shows. He wanted to be in front of the TV in time for a Sunday afternoon kickoff for once.

If he was going to be active on this beautiful autumn morning, he wanted to walk down to the neighborhood coffee shop and order a double espresso with hazelnut syrup and a German pastry guaranteed to melt in his mouth. He wanted God to meet him at the park and talk over life issues.

In fact, Gene wanted the answers to his life issues on a bill-board—enough of this searching stuff. He wanted his dad to be alive again for one more round of golf. He wanted the shape that faced him in the mirror to be thinner right now. He wanted to run the winning touchdown of his last high school game all over again.

But he got up and got dressed anyway. He kissed his wife, woke his kids, and listened to their complaints about how early the wake-up call seemed. After all, he was a dad.

When faith kids become adults, they have to deal with real life as never before. Sometimes that real life is so consuming and tiring that they want to shut themselves off for awhile. It's called "cocooning" and it's a regular phenomenon even among Christians these days.

Still, God's Word stands as the standard for church and home during the adult years—and as a parent, you know you're engaged in a variety of life's big issues simply from your role. You're probably regularly involved with other adults too—neighbors, parents, adult children, or people in a home Bible study.

Never forget: you're a faith kid, too. You need opportunities to be a student as well as a teacher, a receiver as well as a giver. We hope the lists below will help you find and get plugged into a learning situation that meets your needs.

HOW ADULTS LEARN

Adults' lives are marked by:

- transitions
- family involvement
- vocational concerns

You're no exception.

TEACHING DOS AND DON'TS FOR ADULTS

DO

✔ Begin at home; begin a learning project with your spouse.

✔ Look for a group of people who have a sense of community.

✔ Look for a varied group—with a variety of ages and life experiences.

✔ Participate freely in discussion and idea exchange.

✔ Together with other adults, seek to connect the truths of the Bible with everyday life.

✔ Listen attentively to the others in the group; be sensitive to needs and concerns.

✔ Talk about issues that Christians face at any age, while understanding the differences between adult generations.

✔ Honor the unique learning styles of individual adults, especially yours and your spouse's.

✔ Determine a strategy of personal application for your own faith.

DON'T

✘ Don't learn exclusively on your own.

✘ Don't simply acquire content and facts without considering their applications and consequences.

✘ Don't do the same thing over and over again—seek some variety in the way you learn.

✘ Don't underestimate the value of adult generations learning from one another.

✗ Don't dictate to other adults how to apply Bible truth in their lives.

✗ Don't assume that all adults learn in the same way.

Keep On Keeping On

20

"WE ARE HERE TODAY TO ORDAIN YOU to the ministry of the Gospel. . . ."

Mildred and Don watched the ceremony marking the culmination of their son's goal. It was hard not to remember snapshots of all they'd been through raising Steve.

They knew he was precocious as a child, but had to help him handle his tendencies to show off. By the time he was a teenager, he had developed a quick wit—and a quicker mouth—and an even quicker temper.

How do you handle a kid like Steve, with all that potential for good and destruction? For Don, it meant taking time to model ways of handling the hair-trigger temper he'd passed on to his son. It meant hours of showing Steve how to handle an ax and take apart tractor engines and pointing out the wonders of God's creation that could be found on a farm in Iowa. It meant challenging him with stories and books and talking with him away from the distractions of work and school—a lot of one-on-one time spread liberally over the years, even at the cost of another account for Don's insurance business.

Mildred made her impact through a heritage of prayer. Steve saw her begin her day with morning devotions. When he visited his grandparents, he knew where she'd picked up that habit. Mildred showed Steve how to really talk to God—not in a formal, stilted way, but with everyday language.

Don and Mildred rejoiced when Steve made a teenage commitment to Christ. They marveled at his willingness to make his actions match his words. When dating became more of a temptation than a social event for him, he simply quit dating for four months during his senior year of high school and spent Saturday nights at home with them.

They had been the first to help Steve question his call to be in ministry.

Keep On Keeping On

They talked him through his desire to preach and his ego investment in it until his stock answer for "Why be a preacher?" became
a simple sentence: "I want to make a difference for Jesus." They
encouraged, cajoled, challenged theology and word choice, and
honed their son to be the best communicator he could be.

Don and Mildred Wamberg would be the last to tell you they
had somehow "earned" this day. But right now, two decades later,
their son would tell you they earned every minute of that joy and
share in every word he speaks and writes.

You're reading some of them now.

You have everything you need to be a life-changing faith
parent, too.

You have everything you need to make the link between your
home and your child's Sunday School class succeed.

You had what you needed before you picked up this book,
most likely. But just maybe this book has given you a few new
ideas for using what you have.

Your partners in this endeavor are God and the other
people—often Sunday School teachers—who teach your children
faith lessons in many forms.

Your tools to make the home/church link work include your
own faith lessons (planned and spontaneous), a life-linked Bible
lesson at church, its application at home, and your child's return
to that classroom.

You also have a wide range of helpful resources available to you—books, videos, music, toys, games, activity guides—to put together a faith parenting mix that fits your style and your children's needs.

Your strategies to make the most of the home/church link include the following principles:

Teaching Godly Values. The goal of Bible knowledge is life change.

Teachable Moments. Learn to capitalize on—and create—teachable moments with your children.

Identifying Each Child's Needs. The focus of a home lesson is one individual at a time. The focus of a Sunday School lesson is on groups of individuals. When both church and home keep their focus, children can focus too.

Anywhere and Everywhere. Faith parenting can happen in virtually any place and at any time.

Your Indispensable Partner. Like the two wings of an airplane, home and church must be connected in order for a child to soar spiritually.

Growing with Your Children. Faith kids mature at different rates and in different ways; we need to accept those differences, and patiently trust God for the final outcome.

Model Your Faith. Faith parents don't just talk about God—they show their children what God is like.

Be Encouraging. Faith development is a lifelong process; we all need encouragement to keep going.

How Does It Fit? What we teach, and how we teach it, should change as the child develops.

Keep On Keeping On

Your goal, with God's help, is to grow faith kids.

Now you know what they are. Do you know who you are?

You're a faith parent. Remember our definition? *Faith parenting is a fun, effective way to teach godly values to your children—wherever you are—through family reading, personal sharing, playing, and the everyday modeling of God's Word so your children will become faith kids.* If you believe God's Word, you know your example and your words could change your child's life—now and forever.

At the same time, you're a faith kid yourself. You allow Jesus Christ to show in your words and deeds wherever you go—and that starts at home.

You've been doing that for years, too. So keep doing what you've been doing—only better. Use the home/church link that already exists for the sake of your children. Be a faith parent for all it's worth—the fun, the faith lessons, the stories, the games that can make God's Word and ways that much clearer to your children. Teach the faith in the ways only a parent can.

And keep the faith, too.